Young People and the C

The care system looks after the most vulnerable young people in society – those who are, for a variety of reasons, unable to live with their parents. *Young People and the Care Experience* examines what can be done to support young people to remain at home, and if this is not possible, how they can be supported whilst in care and on leaving care. The book explores the range of options – foster care, children's homes and adoption – and how these options interact. Using the latest research and framing the issues through both psycho-social and legal perspectives, the book provides an in-depth analysis of young people's experience of the care system, and how it can be improved.

Examining the challenges faced by children on their journey from initially entering care to living independently after care, the book places these issues in a global context. Specifically, it discusses:

- how to support children and young people at home
- an analysis of the history and demographics of children placed in care
- the challenges faced by children living in foster care
- challenges faced by children living in a children's home
- challenges faced by children being adopted leaving care.

The book will be of interest to all those working with children in care, or those who have experience of the care system as a professional, carer or young person. It will also be of interest to researchers and students of developmental and social psychology, social work, and also to policymakers.

Julie Shaw is a lecturer in Social Work at the University of Lincoln. She recently completed her PhD in Criminology and Social Policy at Leeds Metropolitan University, undertaking research into why children and young people in residential children's homes come to the attention of the youth justice system. Julie has previously worked as court liaison officer for a youth offending team and as a probation officer for a community sentences team.

Nick Frost is Professor of Social Work (Childhood, children and families), at the Faculty of Health, Leeds Metropolitan University. He has researched in the fields of child welfare, family support, children in care and integrated working. Nick worked in local authority social work for 15 years before commencing his academic career.

Adolescence and Society

Series Editor: John C. Coleman

Department of Education, University of Oxford

In the 20 years since it began, this series has published some of the key texts in the field of adolescent studies. The series has covered a very wide range of subjects, almost all of them being of central concern to students, researchers and practitioners. A mark of its success is that a number of books have gone to second and third editions, illustrating its popularity and reputation.

The primary aim of the series is to make accessible to the widest possible readership important and topical evidence relating to adolescent development. Much of this material is published in relatively inaccessible professional journals, and the objective of the books has been to summarise, review and place in context current work in the field, so as to interest and engage both an undergraduate and a professional audience.

The intention of the authors is to raise the profile of adolescent studies among professionals and in institutions of higher education. By publishing relatively short, readable books on topics of current interest to do with youth and society, the series makes people more aware of the relevance of the subject of adolescence to a wide range of social concerns.

The books do not put forward any one theoretical viewpoint. The authors outline the most prominent theories in the field and include a balanced and critical assessment of each of these. Whilst some of the books may have a clinical or applied slant, the majority concentrate on normal development.

The readership rests primarily in two major areas: the undergraduate market, particularly in the fields of psychology, sociology and education; and the professional training market, with particular emphasis on social work, clinical and educational psychology, counselling, youth work, nursing and teacher training.

Also in this series:

Young People and the Care Experience

Research, policy and practice

Julie Shaw and Nick Frost

Routledge
Taylor & Francis Group

LONDON AND NEW YORK

First published 2013
by Routledge
27 Church Road, Hove, East Sussex BN3 2FA

Simultaneously published in the USA and Canada
by Routledge
711 Third Avenue, New York, NY 10017

Routledge is an imprint of the Taylor & Francis Group, an informa business

British Library Cataloguing in Publication Data
A catalogue record for this book is available from the British Library

Library of Congress Cataloging in Publication Data
Shaw, Julie, 1945-
Young people and the care experience : research, policy and practice / Julie
Shaw & Nick Frost.
pages cm
Includes bibliographical references.
ISBN 978-0-415-66522-3 (hbk.) -- ISBN 978-0-415-66526-1 (pbk.) -- ISBN
978-0-203-63049-5 (ebk.) (print) 1. Adoption. 2. Foster home care. 3.
Children--Institutional care. 4. Child care. 5. Child welfare. I. Frost, Nick,
1953- II. Title.
HV875.S4763 2013
362.73--dc23
2012038811

ISBN: 978-0-415-66522-3 (hbk)
ISBN: 978-0-415-66526-1 (pbk)
ISBN: 978-0-20363-049-5 (ebk)

Typeset in Times
by Saxon Graphics Ltd, Derby

MIX
Paper from
responsible sources
FSC
www.fsc.org   FSC® C018575   Printed and bound in Great Britain by MPG Printgroup

Contents

Acknowledgements

We would like to thank the young people in care we have both worked with in helping to shape the material in this book. They often demonstrate good humour and resilience in the most challenging of situations.

Introduction

> You go through care and there are good things and bad things, but we wouldn't be where we are now without some of the bad things. What makes us what we are, which is that we have all come out on top.
>
> (Chelsea, in care 1990s and 2000s)

The aim of this book is to explore the issues and challenges facing children and young people who have experience of the care system. Its focus is on young persons' experiences of care looking at the professional systems, skills and knowledge required to work effectively with young people. We draw on social history, social theory, law and psycho-social theory in attempting to shed light on the operation and outcomes of the care system. The book aims to be comprehensive in examining the full scale of the system – from prevention via the exploration of differing care placements through to routes out of care. Whilst both the authors are grounded in the English care system, wherever possible international material will be drawn on, with a global perspective provided in Chapter 8. Each chapter commences with a direct quote taken from young people interviewed for a recent project undertaken by one of the authors.

The book utilises social theories, policy analysis, research reports and practice material to form a comprehensive, contemporary and critical examination of the care system. We focus on the experiences of young people in the care system – that complex amalgam of family support, foster care, institutional care, adoption and leaving care – that attempts to look after children and young people who are unable to be cared for by their birth parents(s). As a result children and young people in the care system have a unique relationship with the state:

> The vast majority of children enter care for reasons associated with neglect and abuse and not through any action of their own. When the state decides to take on the responsibility for parenting children who

cannot live safely with their birth family, it creates a unique relationship between the child and the state-as-parent that is not replicated elsewhere in the many relationships that exist between citizens and their government. (National Care Advisory Service *et al.*, 2012, p. 4)

The nature of this 'unique relationship' will be explored in all the chapters. The focus of this series is on the adolescent or young person, and therefore this book mainly considers the experiences of this group of young people. However, it should be noted that young people will often have earlier contact with the care system as young children, for example, by being adopted as a baby. It is also the case that some youthful parents may have experience of the care system being utilised for their own children. We therefore necessarily employ a wide lens in examining the experiences of children and young people of all ages.

At first sight the care system may seem to concern only a small minority of young people: in recent years, for example, there have been around 60,000 children and young people in care at any one time out of around 11 million people under 18 in England. However, there are number of reasons for recognising that the 'reach' of the care system is much wider than that approximate 60,000 figure.

First, the 60,000 figure is a 'snapshot' – it records only the number of young people in care at any one time – in the English case that is on the 31 March each year: it therefore does not reflect turnover, or 'churn' in the system. Young people come in and out of care and therefore there is a constant change in composition which is not reflected in the 'snapshot' figure.

Second, young people not actually in the care system may be affected by it. Such groups would include the siblings of young people in care and the birth children of foster carers and adopters. In this sense the 'reach' and impact of the care system is much wider than the 60,000 who appear in official statistics.

Third, and more theoretically, the care system has an impact on us all as it represents a key relationship between the state and the family. The care system raises fundamental questions such as:

- When should the state intervene in the family?
- What responsibilities should the state have for children and young people who are unable to live with their birth families?
- Can the state provide 'good enough' parenting for separated children?

Thus the care system is in a sense 'everybody's business' as it has an impact on how we address some of the most fundamental social challenges of contemporary society.

We hope to shed light on these issues in the book.

The focus then is on 'young people' who live in the 'care system'. The terms we have used so far raise a number of challenges about the use of language and concepts. Whilst these terminological debates can sometimes seem rather obscure, arguably, the use of terms really matters ashow they are deployed helps shape attitudes and professional practice.

First of all, looking at the use of the terms 'children' and 'young people'. In this book we use 'children' to refer to younger children – whilst there is no strict definition, we are generally referring to those under about 11. Such children will be largely dependent on their carers for all their needs, whether physical or emotional. In contrast we use the term 'young people' to refer to people aged approximately 11 and over. These young people have entered their 'transition to adulthood' – where they will be increasingly able to care for themselves, will usually develop strong peer groups and will be able to take more and more control of their own lives.

One important point underlying the whole discussion is that assessment of individual situations and genuine participation by children and young people should be an essential element of the care system. Therefore, it follows that there is no easy blueprint that points to a given approach being best for, say, all 14-year-olds. Care needs to be taken to address the unique needs of each child or young person, in an age and development-appropriate manner.

It is the 'young people' group who are the primary focus of this book, and indeed this series. Thus we focus largely on topics such as children's homes and leaving care which are issues for 'young people' in the care system. However the 'real life' situation is, of course, more complex. For example, a 17-year-old may have entered the care system as a baby, or indeed a teenager in care may have a baby themselves. For these reasons we have taken a holistic approach – and the entire book should provide a lens for looking at the care system as a whole.

Another terminological issue is how we refer to children and young people who live within the care system. We discuss how some terms differ internationally in our chapter on global approaches. In the United Kingdom two terms tend to be used either 'in care', or 'looked after' children and young people, sometimes abbreviated to LAC (looked-after children). 'Children in care' is a longstanding term – see Jean Heywood's classic book *Children in Care*, for example, which was first published in 1965. Following the Children Act 1989 children began to be referred to as being 'looked after' (following, e.g., section 22 of the Act). During the twenty-firstcentury both terms ('children in care' and 'looked after children') have been used interchangeably, with the abbreviation LAC being used widely in professional discourse. In this context we prefer the term 'care system' to describe the whole range of placements for children and young people and 'children in care' or 'young people in care' when we are referring to actual people.

The structure of the book follows a journey through the care system – from life with birth family, via foster care, children's homes and adoption, through to 'ageing out of care'. Whilst no specific young person is likely to follow this exact sequence it does reflect a range of options and routes within the care system.

In Chapter 1 we start with an analysis of what happens to children and young people before they enter the care system and whether we can prevent reception into the care system. We explore issues around what is called 'family support', sometimes referred to as 'prevention', 'early help' or 'early intervention'. It is argued that we cannot understand the care system without examining the 'gateway' to the care system and how this is planned, managed and delivered. A wide range of theories and research findings will be outlined that help us understand family support.

In Chapter 2 we go on to consider who is in care and explore the settings in which they live. This chapter provides an historical perspective on the emergence of the care system, thus providing a crucial roadmap explaining how the care system has been shaped by the past. It will be argued that many historical features of the care system are still with us today. By providing a brief historical overview of the development of the care system and the factors (social, ideological, political and financial) which have contributed both to the nature of the provision on offer and those who are targeted for intervention we will explore how issues such as low expectations for children in care, are still with us today. We then proceed to explore the make-up of the current care population, including who is currently in care, their demographic profile, and the nature of their placements. This will be placed in the context of contemporary legislation, policy and professional procedure.

In Chapter 3 we explore the part of the system which is statistically dominant in most parts of the world – foster care. This is care provided in private domestic settings within or outside of kinship networks. It is now, in many countries, the mainstay of the care system. The majority of children in care live in foster care. Being reflective of the 'conventional' family this is popularly thought to provide the crucial mechanism for providing better life chances for children and young people. The plethora of recent research on foster care is presented and analysed, along with consideration of issues around race and gender in foster care and the recent proliferation of intensive foster care programmes.

Foster care exists, as explained in Chapter 3, in many forms across the globe – it varies in terms of how far it is regulated and in terms of the emphasis on 'kinship' care as opposed to 'stranger' care. It also tends to exist in some form of tension with residential care, which we explore in Chapter 4.

Foster care has a long history – examples of children living with people who are not their birth parents can be found in the historical and literary accounts going back many centuries. In modern terms the history of foster care can be usefully traced to the Second World War – evacuee children were effectively 'fostered' with often unrelated strangers far from their homes and their birth families. As is often the case major wars lead to significant changes to social policy – and the Second World War triggered many such changes, epitomised in the United Kingdom in the 1948 Children Act. That Act reflected in general terms social changes brought about by the experience of global war but also specifically lessons learned from the death of a young person in foster care – Denis O'Neill (Frost and Stein, 1989).

Chapter 4 explores the system of care which was widespread in the Western world until the challenge to institutional care that took place in the 1960s and 1970s – children's homes and other forms of institutional care. It is important to recognise that in some countries (e.g. Bulgaria) this remains a dominant form of providing for children separated from their birth families. The residential care system has in many parts of the world experienced major change and reform in the aftermath of 'scandals' about abuse in residential care. In this chapter however we also provide a positive perspective on the achievements of the residential care system, exploring the current role and function of the residual children's home sector, touching on relevant theoretical perspectives, as well as the increasingly important role of the private sector and looking at issues faced by children and young people who live in children's homes, including relationships with staff and other residents, the potential impact of institutional regimes and involvement with the criminal justice system, as well as the impact of overarching systemic factors such as being placed 'out of area', or having multiple placements. This chapter draws on recent doctoral research by one of the authors (Shaw, 2010), as well as that of others in the field.

Chapter 5 explores the process of 'being adopted' and the various challenges and controversies that face adoption policy and practice. It will be argued that adoption presents many of the controversies that exist in relation to childhood in the twenty-first century - what should the family look like, when should the state intervene in the family and what does child care practice look like in an ethnically divided society? The chapter utilises a recently-published influential English report (Narey, 2011) to provide a structure and narrative. The discussion concludes with an extended examination of the highly controversial issues around trans-racial adoption, and the practice implications of these debates.

Chapter 6 explores the issue of 'ageing out of care' or 'leaving care' and how young people can best be prepared and supported through the process of transition. The chapter provides an important discussion of the role of planning in the care system and how young people can be fully involved in this process. It argues that 'leaving care' is in many ways the 'acid test' of the care system – can the care system deliver effective outcomes for the children and young people it 'looks after'?

Chapter 7 takes a global perspective on being in care and explores differing global experiences. Of course we cannot provide a comprehensive analysis of every nation – but we draw on some specific material to illustrate dominant global trends and directions. In particular we explore the role of the social pedagogue, which provides a potential international model for improving the care system. We also look at research that compares the care experience across 12 European and central Asian countries – as an exemplar of attempting to understand global trends in the care system.

Chapter 8 examines two key outcomes for children and young people. We have explored two key outcomes here – health and education, which tend to underpin life opportunities later in life. People entering the care system are likely to be disadvantaged in these two fields when they enter care and it is a test of the care system if it is able to deliver better outcomes for young people in these fields. The chapter explores how good effective practice can improve outcomes and assesses policy and research in relation to these outcomes.

The final chapter draws on our previous work to speculate on the future of the care system and what this might look like. What is the future of the system that cares for looked after children and young people? Drawing on our data and arguments we suggest how the system could be improved and reformed.

We hope that the book will be of interest to a wide range of people.

In recent years there has been an increasing focus on multi-disciplinary work with children and young people in care, resulting in a need for greater awareness of the issues among professionals such as teachers, youth workers and health professionals. We hope that students on a range of courses will alos find the book of interest. This may include:

- undergraduates: on social work and related professional courses
- Postgraduate students: on professional qualifying and post-qualifying courses
- professionals working with children and young people in a number of settings
- the academic and research community
- lay people who may, for a variety of reasons, have an interest in the care system.

The profile of children and young people in the care system has become heightened in recent years and a wide range of professionals are now engaged in work with this group. The public and political profile around the issues has been both emphasised and increased by the extensive press coverage about abuse in care, deaths of children who arguably should have been in care, around who should be able to adopt and, perhaps, most of all, around race, ethnicity and adoption. We hope to contribute to these debates and controversies.

The book is planned and structured so that each chapter is free-standing – in the sense that the reader may wish to read one chapter in order to gain an understanding of a specific issue. For example, the chapter on adoption can be read and understood independently for the reader wishing to focus on this particular topic.

1 Supporting children and young people at home

Prevention, family support and the care system

> I lived with different parts of the family. I loved it at granddad's cos he brought me up.
>
> Laura, in care late 1990s and 2000s

It is not possible to examine the care system without looking at the available support in the community, which often has a stated and explicit aim of preventing the reception of young people into the care system. Family support for children living at home will be examined and critically analysed, and its relationship to the care system considered. The usefulness and deployment of the concept of 'children on the edge of care' will be explored.

The care system cannot be considered in isolation from the systems of 'family support' that exists in each national situation. The concept of 'family support' varies considerably in each nation but usually has a link with the care system through being conceived as preventing the need for reception into care. The structure of the care population is therefore partially structured by the nature of the family support system: theoretically, at least, the number of children in care will depend at least to some extent, on the effectiveness of the family support system.

'Family support'

'Family support' comprises a range of differing practices and theories and thus it is difficult to both define and theorise. Family support may be community-based or centre-based, it can be highly professionalised or sometimes it can draw mainly on volunteers, it may be inspired by community development or therapeutic principles. For these reasons family support can be seen as a 'slippery concept' (Frost, 2003, p. 7) or as containing so many meanings 'it is difficult to disentangle them' (Penn and Gough, 2002, p. 17).

Despite the multi-faceted and wide-ranging nature of family support it has a key role within the child welfare system as a whole and an intimate connection with the care system in particular. In many social and political systems family support is based in a legislative framework which draws on the United Nations Convention on the Rights of the Child: 'Children should not be separated from their parents unless it is for their *own good* (UNICEF, 2011).

As we have seen, the care system occupies a complex social space between the state and the family, in some ways family support and ideas about 'early intervention' (Allen, 2011) also suggest controversial theoretical challenges about the relationship between childhood, families and the state (Frost, 2011).

No state system wants large numbers of young people 'in care', for a series of practical, economic and political reasons. The care system is expensive to operate and is often perceived as having negative outcomes. Thus it follows that governments would want to do what they can to offer family support, with the aim of minimising the number of children in care. However there are a number of barriers that present themselves:

- Family support requires investment. A comprehensive family support system arguably existed in some totalitarian societies (the Soviet Union in the 1930s, Cuba in the 1960s and China during the early years of their socialist revolution) but these were expensive systems, driven by investment in services and in these contexts had authoritarian overtones (see a fascinating discussion by Bronfenbrenner (1974) comparing the US and Soviet Union).
- The technology of family support is uncertain: in other words the operation of family support raises the 'what works?' problem. Should a given society invest in large universal programmes or more specific, targeted programmes, or a mix of the two? Whilst research is suggestive (see Allen, 2011) it is too uncertain to give definitive responses.

There are also ideological challenges. Fox-Harding (1991) has outlined the differing ideological stances the state can take towards family policy:

- The *laissez faire* approach – largely leaving the family to be self-regulating and self-monitoring, within the normal parameters of the law. This is a low investment, but high-risk position.
- A *parental rights/family support* stance which emphasises the rights of the parent to raise their own children, and offers support in carrying out this task. This position is 'pro-family', and suggests some investment in supportive services.
- A *protectionist* stance where the state places an emphasis on ensuring children are safeguarded from parental abuse and violence. This position

suggests some investment in protection services and has political costs in terms of being potentially seen as undermining family autonomy.

• A *children's rights* position where the focus is on the child and their need to be full participants in their own lives. (Fox-Harding, 1991)

An example of a specific ideological stance is provided by communitarianism which offers an approach to family support which perhaps reflects the second, parental rights position in the Fox-Harding framework. Communitarians argue for a partnership between state and family with rights and responsibilities on each side of the equation. This position was extremely influential during the periods in office of both the Blair British government and Clinton US administration (Driver and Martell, 1997). Two academics, one on each side of the Atlantic, were particularly influential in terms of communitarian thinking – Anthony Giddens (1998 in the United Kingdom and the theorist Amitai Etzioni (1993) in the United States. The latter represents a trend within communitarianism that places a strong emphasis on the responsibilities of parents in raising their children. Etzioni states that: 'Making a child is a moral act. Obviously it obligates the parents to the child. But it also obligates the parents to the community' (1993, p. 54).

This is clearly relevant to the care system – it asks the parent to take their responsibilities seriously and thus to ensure that they do everything that is possible to raise their own children. Etzioni argues that the needs of children should be prioritised over the needs of adults: 'parents have a moral responsibility to the community to invest themselves in the proper upbringing of their children, and communities – to enable parents to so dedicate themselves'(1993, p. 54). Giddens argues that the state has a more prominent role in family support than that proposed by Etzioni.

Communitarianism therefore provides a potential framework for reflecting on how the state and the family relate to each other, and the crucial role that family support practice has at the interface between the two. The British version of communitarianism embodied by then Prime Minister Tony Blair took the form of many state-led initiatives such as Sure Start, a locally-based family support programme, and Child Trust Funds, which encouraged financial saving in children's names.

Family support: a theoretical and research base

The effectiveness of family support is difficult to measure and researchers have struggled to demonstrate its impact (see Rutter, 2007). Perhaps the pre-eminent example of a positive impact is the widely acknowledged United States project known as the High/Scope Perry Pre-School Program. The programme operated in an inner city area of Michigan in the United States during the 1960s. It consisted of a family support programme that worked with African American children aged between three and five. The programme was made up of two-and-half hours per day of centre-based day care for the children during the week, which drew on an active learning model. This day care was supplemented by a home visiting process. The programme itself was similar to many projects that operate around the world but what makes the project stand out is that it was accompanied by an extensive research project which followed up the children at 15, 19, 27 and 40 years of age. The children involved in the study were allocated to the intervention group, High Scope group and a control group: there were 58 children in the intervention group and 63 in the control. The dropout rate is notably low for such an ambitious study with the researchers being in contact with around 90 per cent of the group at the 40th birthday follow up.

The findings of the High/Scope Perry research have been extensively reported. The data analysis is both complex and sophisticated and, in some respects, very much contested.

Using the High Scope data, Heckman and colleagues undertook a secondary analysis of the statistics, which is critical of some of the original research methods, but they nevertheless conclude that, 'crime reduction is a major benefit of this program' (Heckman *et al.*, 2009, p. 11). An example of the facts that back up this assertion include the following:

> The program group had fewer arrests overall than the control group (averages of 1.3 versus 2.3 arrests per person), fewer felony arrests (averages of 0.7 v. 2.0 arrests per person), and fewer juvenile court petitions filed (averages of 0.2 v. 0.4 petitions per person). (Parks, 2000, p. 2)

This is highly relevant to this book as the youth crime system is a major entry point to institutional care in the United States, particularly for black youth. Bellfield *et al.* (2006) undertook a cost benefit analysis of this data and make an estimate that $12.90 was saved from the public purse for every single dollar invested in High/Scope Perry arguing that these gains came mainly from reduced crime by males. Cunha and Heckman (2006), drawing from this High/Scope Perry Pre-School Program data and from other programme data argue that: 'the most effective supplements supply family resources to young children from disadvantaged environments' (2006, p. 1).

This data, therefore, provides strong evidence to establish the efficacy of family support programmes. Many of the analysts, including Cunha and Heckman, argue the social gains are related to educational change so that, using American terminology: 'completing high school is a major crime prevention strategy' (2006, p. 60).

Whilst the data presented here seems to be very persuasive, the impact of such programmes remains a topic of debate and controversy – as with many issues discussed in this book. This point is clearly demonstrated by the arguments emerging from the High/Scope Perry Pre-School Programme evidence. Indeed one commentator asserts that as a result of High/Scope Perry Pre-School Programme:

> ... the children from this program have in reality become welfare moms and hardened criminals
>
> (Idaho Coalition of Home Educators,
> www.iche-idaho.org/issues/34)

This position draws on the same data discussed by Bellfield, Heckman and others: it reflects the powerful impact of ideology and how perspectives are influenced by the differing value positions outlined by Fox-Harding (1991) and discussed earlier in this chapter.

Despite the differences and controversies it is indisputable that the US research base is extensive, which is certainly in contrast with the research profile of other parts of the world. The English Social Care Institute for Excellence (SCIE), for example, argues that:

> primary research in the areas of early intervention and of integrated working are in their infancy, and there is, therefore, limited direct evidence. (2007, p. 3)

The evidence challenges in relation to family support were illustrated by the experience of evaluating Sure Start – which was powerfully critiqued by Sir Michael Rutter (2006). The evaluation evidence was mixed, with some negative impacts being identified following Sure Start intervention. Rutter argues that the entire Sure Start enterprise was flawed as the way in which each local programme was undertaken varied considerably thus making the research task a very complex undertaking. We can see therefore that the exact nature of family support is difficult to research and analyse and that the exact relationship with the care system remains uncertain. We return to this question throughout this book.

Theoretical approaches to family support

Having outlined some of the research findings relating to family support, we now move on to explore its theoretical base. In the presentation of the High/Scope Perry programme data earlier in this chapter we see some of the features that are required to help us build a theory of family support and how it may contribute to preventing children and young people coming into care. Family support, it can be argued, has the following characteristics:

- family support is based on the idea of 'early intervention'. This means that programmes can be relevant early in the life of the child or early in the emergence of the identified social issue in the family. Thus family support can be relevant to young people, and not only to young children, for example by addressing children on the 'edge of care'.
- family support is a pro-active process which engages with the parent and/or young person in the process of change. It suggests active attempts to bring about change by the worker and the family network.
- family support attempts to prevent the emergence of family and social problems and to promote better outcomes for young people through family coherence.
- family support is based on theories of change. The aim of any intervention is to result in some desirable change and is based in a belief that change is achievable.
- family support generates wider social benefits. Such benefits may be savings in public expenditure, decreases in social problems or a reduction in the number of children coming into care (see Allen, 2011).

The English National Family and Parenting Institute (NFPI) has identified four principles of family support which reflect our discussion above. The NFPI argues that:

There is no single policy that can meet the many needs of Britain's families. And help needs to be sensitive to the subtle distinctions in people's feelings and values. A balance between the needs of children and the broader needs of families should be maintained; although in many areas they are indistinguishable, it is important that children's separate needs are not marginalized.

And further that, 'Public policy to support families needs to be universal, non-stigmatising, wide-ranging and accessible'.

The four principles the NFPI identify are as follows:

'*Support for all families*

Government services exist to support parents and families to lead a decent life, and raise their children. A large body of research into the direct needs of families shows that all families need access to support during the course of a child's life and that support services should be available as other universal services which we take for granted. Universal support needs to be supplemented by services targeted at those in greatest need.

No stigma attached

Raising children is not the sole responsibility of the individual parents. Parents must rely on others, both from their families and from outside the home. It is a task for the whole community. People who use services should be seen as valued users, rather than passive recipients of services. There is no stigma to asking for services or for help. How, for example, can disabled parents find the support they need without their children being labelled 'in need' by local social services departments?

Support across the board

Services must be wide-ranging and overlapping. Measurement of success is not always possible, and services that are easily measured may not always be the best option. Services supporting families range from supporting couples' relationships, direct services for children and young people, play, youth and leisure services, transport, fiscal policy, housing and education policy, as well as direct services to help families. The Government must work hand-in-hand with local authorities and the voluntary sector, who are providing many innovative and effective ways of helping parents. Cross-cutting and multi-agency work must become the norm.

Accessible

Accessible services means thinking creatively about providing or enabling affordable help. Informal ways of helping parents can play as important a role as voluntary or statutory provision. Accessibility also means easy access to information about services and information about parenting issues which encourage parents to find their own solutions and help. A willingness to think creatively about sources of support and advice can lead to other solutions than simply calling for more of the same. Supporting existing community and faith-based organisations to provide support opens other doors to parents.'
(NFPI, 2001)

The Centre For Excellence and Outcomes (C4EO) report 'Grasping the nettle: early intervention for children, families and communities' (2011) takes a similar approach to that taken by the NFPI but uses a more explicit research-driven approach to identify what they call the 'five golden threads' that should form the basis of early intervention. These are described as follows:

- the best start in life
- language for life
- engaging parents
- smarter working, better services
- knowledge is power.

Let us examine each of these in turn.

The 'best start *in life*' refers to the importance of early child development, which includes pre-birth experiences. This clearly points to the importance of making sure that the early years are supported by services as fully as possible. The C4EO point to the importance of children's centres and ensuring that they reach the most vulnerable; the importance of breast feeding; and the crucial role of volunteer and peer support for new parents.

'Language for life' places an emphasis on the importance of communication skills to be successful. The report points to the link between poor language skills and poor childhood outcomes; the need for a higher policy profile for communication issues; the importance of addressing language delay; the key role of the professional workforce; and the need to boost professional and parental skills through training programmes.

'Engaging parents', the report argues, is crucial to the concept of early intervention, citing research evidence as supporting the positive engagement of parents 'in a collaborative approach, building on their strengths and taking into account their views and experiences'" (2011, p. 7).

'Smarter working, better services' highlights the importance of well-designed services in delivering early support. The report highlights the role of effective leadership of services; effective commissioning of services; the need for ongoing support; the importance of multi-agency working; the importance of assessing any needs; and the need to require professional skills.

Finally, the 'Grasping the Nettle' report argues that 'Knowledge is power'. By this they mean that there is a need to use research and data effectively to support and inform the delivery of services.

Here we can see two differing, but complementary, approaches presented by the NFPI and the C4EO to understanding the role of family support or early intervention in preventing family problems either emerging or deteriorating. There can be little doubt, given the research evidence, that if an effective family support system was in place the number of children in care would decline and that the quality of life of children and young people would improve.

Delivering family support

One of the key issues regarding family support is the means by which it is actually delivered to families in need. Such programmes can be delivered on many levels, all of which may help to reduce the number of children who enter the care system. The most universal services are those which exist on a state-wide basis. Many of these form part of the landscape of everyday life, such as universal child benefit, and are not always considered as part of family support programmes as such. These include programmes intended to reduce child poverty (such as child tax credits) or political programmes which have fundamentally attempted to change childhood. There are examples where the reform of childhood has been a fundamental aim of states – such as in post-revolutionary Soviet Union (Bronfenbrenner, 1974) or China (Xhou and Hou, 1999). These state policies were effectively attempting to provide what may be conceptualised as profound and over-arching 'family support' programmes, which were explicitly political and ideological in nature.

Programmes which are more usually seen as family support schemes are those which are community-based or neighbourhood initiatives. Examples include Sure Start in the United Kingdom (Belsky *et al.* 2007 and Rutter, 2007), or High/Scope in the United States, as seen above (Bellfield *et al.* 2006). These initiatives often have community-wide aims to improve and support family life in defined geographical areas, often areas which have been identified as disadvantaged.

Other family support initiatives, such as parenting programmes or those designed to tackle key challenges such as domestic violence or substance abuse, in contrast to state-wide or neighbourhood projects, tend to focus on families that already have identified problems. These may include treatment programmes or those programmes aimed at bringing about change in family behaviour or functioning. Again these are important initiatives which may, if successful, reduce the need to bring children into care.

Thus we can see that one way that family support can be understood is by utilising this typology: state-wide; community; or family-based.

More traditionally family support is understood in terms of the aims, or level, of the intervention. Such early intervention programmes tend to be identified using three levels, drawing on early models developed by Hardiker *et al.* (1991). This typology of primary, secondary and tertiary prevention is defined below.

Primary prevention usually consists of universal programmes, often area-based, working on a voluntary basis with a wide range of families. There is usually no stigma attached to using such services and the aim can be seen as preventing the emergence of family problems. Examples of primary prevention projects may include adventure playgrounds, toy libraries and children's centres.

Secondary prevention is usually aimed at families with existing challenges, who usually recognise these issues themselves and who wish to work with agencies towards change through a support and partnership model. Examples of secondary prevention may include volunteer home visiting programmes such as Home Start.

Tertiary prevention is conceptualised as being at the 'heavier' or perhaps more intensive end of a family support spectrum, and thus may focus on issues such as drug and alcohol misuse or domestic violence. Tertiary prevention may involve working with children on the 'edge of care' (see discussion later in this chapter) or with children and young people returning home to their birth parents following a period in care.

We can see then that there is interplay between the location of the intervention (state, community or family) and the level of intervention (primary, secondary or tertiary) which is represented diagrammatically in Figure 1.

	primary	*secondary*	*tertiary*
initiative			
state-wide	parenting help lines	mediation schemes	
community-based	play schemes children's centres	targeted work in children's centres	domestic violence programmes
family-centred	advice 'drop-ins' parenting advice/training	home start and related home visiting schemes	family intervention projects

Figure 1 A matrix of family support interventions (adapted from Frost and Dolan, in Davies 2012)

Gilligan (2000) develops the idea of family support existing at different levels and argues that this diverse and uncertain deployment of the term can be best seen as existing in three forms:

- *Developmental Family Support*: building universal services locally to support all children and families.
- *Compensatory Family Support*: seeking to support disadvantaged families through special provision.
- *Protective Family Support*: seeking to strengthen the coping and resilience of individual families. (2000, p. 15)

Developmental family support can be seen as similar to the universal services discussed above that can be used without stigma by wide sections of the population – they might include school-based services, such as breakfast clubs, and services such as national helplines.

Compensatory family support is more explicitly targeted than development family support. These services may exist specifically in poorer areas in order to challenge the impact of social inequities, and might include home visiting, respite care, and centre-based activities such as parenting classes.

Protective family support exists to address high levels of need. Gilligan describes it as follows:

> to promote the child's safety and development and prevent the child leaving the family by reducing stressors in the child's and family's life, promoting competence in the child, connecting the child and family members to relevant supports and resources and promoting morale and competence in parents. (2000, p. 14)

We can see therefore that, as stated at the start of this chapter, family support is difficult to define and conceptualise. Underpinning all family support initiatives, however conceptualised, is a value base that suggests that social problems can be minimised and that this may in turn contribute to reducing the number of children in care.

Children on the edge of care

Thus far we have examined the crucial role of family support in enabling and supporting families in raising their own children. These arguments apply to whole populations and include universal services. Now we turn to exploring the concept of children on 'the edge of care' and how services can work with this targeted group of young people, who are the main focus of this book.

The concept of 'children on the edge of care' refers to those children and young people who are identified as being in real and imminent risk of entering the care system. The children, young people and their families require assistance if they are to avoid reception into care.

The English official inspectoral body, Ofsted (the Office for Standards in Education, Children's Services and Skills), undertook a study that involved interviews with 39 young people and 33 parents/carers that were identified as falling into the category that the children were on the 'edge of care' (Ofsted, 2011a). The report is very positive about the potential impact of services:

> Without exception, all the young people and parents spoken to were very clear about the difference the support had made to their lives. For

some the impact had been significant and they felt that their lives had been turned around. (2011a, p. 12)

Many of the young people were judged to have been living in 'poor home conditions, often for long periods in time' (2011a, p. 13).The outcomes, in terms of avoiding care, were successful in all the studied cases. The report concludes that 'it was the quality of the professional involved, significantly the key professional, which was the crucial factor in helping to achieve success' (2011a, p. 4). The services had the following features:

- Strong multi-agency working both operationally and strategically.
- Clear and consistent referral pathways.
- Clearly understood and consistent decision-making processes based on thorough assessment of risks and strengths of the family network.
- A prompt, persistent, and flexible approach, based on listening to the views of the young person and the family and building on their strengths.
- A clear plan of work based on thorough assessment and mutually agreed goals: regular review of progress and risk factors; robust and understood arrangements between agencies in respect of risk management; and clear planning for case closure and for sustainability of good outcomes (2011a, p. 5)

We can see then a clearly conceptualised and well-resourced system can potentially help in working with children on the 'edge of care'.

Conclusion

This chapter has explored the interface between family support systems and the care system. It has argued that investment in family support helps to shape and influence the nature of the care system and when and whether young people enter the care system. The evidence base seems to be persuasive that investment in family support will pay dividends both in terms of preventing family breakdown and in financial terms. In designing care systems policymakers therefore also need to pay attention to designing effective family support systems. The interface between the two is crucial in promoting the best interests of children and young people. Having explored the family support system we can go on to examine disparate elements of the care system, commencing with a wide-ranging view of the care system and how it is formulated.

2 Who is in care and where do they live?

Understanding the care population

> I went in care at the age of five, and my Mum got a new partner and then they had my sister and it all starting breaking down. I remember there was a woman at the door from social services and all my stuff was packed and I was taken away. I have moved all around Sheffield all my life. I have had loads of foster placements. I really don't know how many off the top of my head, I miscalculate it, it is over 30.
>
> (Myles, in care 1990s and 2000s)

While the focus of this book is primarily on contemporary research, policy and practice, this chapter begins by providing an historical overview of the development of the care system and the factors which have contributed both to the nature of placements and those who are targeted for intervention. It then proceeds to explore the make-up of the current care population and the nature of their placements, before reviewing developments in contemporary policy and practice.

Historical overview

There is little doubt that the socio-economic status of those who have required assistance has been a particularly pertinent influence on child care policy and practice. Frost, Mills and Stein (1999) provide a detailed account of the attempts of the state to regulate the perceived threat posed by the poor and the dispossessed, with specific provision for children and young people beginning to emerge as early as 1536. They describe how various pieces of legislation have been enacted with the aim of dealing with the 'problem' of children and young people who were unable to rely on their families of origin for financial and practical support, and how both the state and the philanthropic sectors have (often in tandem), intervened to provide for their accommodation and 'moral guidance'.

An example of such legislation can be found in the Poor Law Act of 1547, which allowed for the children of established vagrants to be taken into apprenticeships, thus reinforcing one of the main aims of sixteenth-century intervention – to emphasise work and the development of skills to save children and young people from pauperism. Thereafter there was an emerging emphasis on child welfare, with the establishment in 1552 of charitable residential provision aimed specifically at children: but again the key aim of Christ's Hospital was to ensure that the children were educated and able to pursue a trade. According to Frost, Mills and Stein (1999, p. 8), these developments represented, 'an educative model which was designed to train and crucially rescue children from a future of vagrancy'. However, there was 'coercive backup' for this educative ideal: any child attempting to run away being punished and deprived of their liberty. Indeed, the presence of a 'coercive backup' has often been a feature of provision for children and young people who are reliant on the state or charitable provision:

> What we have seen is the inherent tension between 'care' and 'control' – an expressed wish to improve the condition of pauperised children and young people, which exists side by side with punishment, control and containment. (1999, p. 10)

The ideology of 'control' appears to have increased in dominance between the sixteenth and eighteenth centuries, when the Industrial Revolution brought about social and economic upheaval and attention focused on the control of (what were perceived to be) the 'dangerous classes'. This, in turn, had an impact on the way that children were perceived and responded to, producing a shift to more punitive attitudes. In 1834, the Poor Law Amendment Act led to a growth in the number of residential establishments, most of which were 'multi-purpose' workhouses where all paupers were housed together, including children and young people. These establishments were operated in accordance with the principle of 'less eligibility', which came about as part of widespread concern over the able-bodied unemployed, who were often perceived as being the authors of their own misfortunes: lazy and unwilling to earn enough money to support themselves. As a result of this, it was considered that they should be incentivised to seek work and provide for themselves, by ensuring that workhouse conditions were such that only the truly desperate would seek assistance there. This resulted in regimes which enforced harsh and petty rules and regulations: food was to be plain and frugal, inmates were required to undertake repetitive and boring work, they were not allowed to leave without permission, and a ban was imposed on perceived 'luxury' items, including tobacco and spirits. Although children were officially exempt from the principle, they were nevertheless subject to the same regimes, albeit with the provision of compulsory education. Smith describes how, 'the Poor Laws thus embedded punitive and negative images of the poor, in which poverty was individualised and considered in isolation of the social context from which it stemmed' (2009, p. 21).

Indeed, it is of note that none of the policies up to and including this point challenged the status quo in terms of attempting to ameliorate the social and economic circumstances of the families who were unable to look after their children. The focus was at all times on the reformation of the aberrant individual in the hope that in the right environment and with the correct instruction, they would renounce the ways of their parents and lead 'decent', law-abiding lives. As such, it increasingly became perceived as desirable in both the state and philanthropic sectors to remove children from the 'demoralising influences' of older paupers in order to given them a chance of escaping pauperism. Such policies stemmed from negative perceptions of parents who were unable to provide adequate care for their children which, 'applied even when there were obvious and practical reasons for the need for care away from home' (Jackson, 2006, p. 12). Children were therefore separated from their families in the belief that this would improve their chances of a better life. Indeed, 'children who were received into care were rarely returned to their parents and continuing contact between them was rare; ties were often permanently severed' (Hannon, Wood and Bazalgette, 2010, p. 44). One of the most notorious policies of severance which was pursued right up to the 1960s, was the practice of sending large numbers of children to Australia or Canada, many of whom were then subjected to abuse and exploitation (Bean and Melville, 1990).

The official dominance of the 'less eligibility' principle continued until the early twentieth century, when, 'a number of surveys and reports pointed to the widespread nature of poverty and suggested that the causes lay outside of individual failure and pathology, thereby beginning to discredit the Poor Law' (Frost, Mills and Stein 1999, pp. 18–9). Nevertheless, Jackson highlights how:

> Long after workhouses – at least under that name – had disappeared, the idea of 'less eligibility', that provision for children in care should never be better than they might [have] enjoyed in their family and class of origin, maintained a strong influence on the thinking of policy makers and administrators.' (2006, p. 11)

Indeed, such attitudes were in evidence among certain professionals in the care system who were interviewed as part of the author's PhD research where some expressed concern that the young people should not be given unrealistic expectations of the 'reality' of life after leaving care by the provision of too generous an allowance or too many expensive outings or holidays (see Shaw, 2010).

However, 'the aftermath of the Second World War and the acknowledgement of the disruption of family life caused by evacuation prompted social reformers to take stock of provision for children' (Smith, 2009, p. 25). The death of a child, Denis O'Neill, beaten and starved to death in 1945 in a foster home which had been subject only to cursory inspection, prompted a wholesale review of the care system. The Curtis Report of 1946 set out the basic form of the present care system and the principles underlying it, including the ideal of bringing up each child in a manner resembling as closely as possible ordinary family life. It was critical of large-scale institutional living and proposed that children and young people should be provided for in smaller units (of around 20 children) located nearer to population centres. The report laid great emphasis on the need to treat each child/young person as an individual, in contrast to the institutional nature of most child care at the time and, 'came down firmly in favour of foster care as preferable to children's homes and urged local authorities to make a "vigorous effort" to extend the system' (Jackson, 2006, p. 13). Smith (2009) highlights how the child guidance movement, drawing on Freudian psychology and emphasising the importance of working with children in the context of their family relationships, was a powerful influence on the thinking of the time. Nevertheless, children and young people continued to be accommodated primarily in institutional settings for a number of years.

The subsequent Children Act 1948 established local authority children's departments as the first professional social work service for children and young people in the United Kingdom. Children's departments were initially quite small organisations and the children's officers, 'took a keen personal interest in every child in care, most of whom they knew individually' (Jackson, 2006, p. 14). The departments ran their own residential establishments and employed fostering and adoption officers to families for orphaned, neglected and abused children and young people. Section 12(1) of the Act states that:

> Where a child is in the care of a local authority it shall be the duty of that authority to exercise their powers with respect to him so as to further his best interests; and to afford him opportunity for the proper development of his character and abilities.

Here, there appears to be official acknowledgement that, in theory at least, the child in care is an individual with a distinct personality and needs, rather than belonging to a homogenous group which simply requires management and control. The Act also placed a duty on local authorities to restore the child to their family wherever possible, thus breaking with the child rescue ideology of earlier times. This theme continued when, in 1952, the Association of Children's Officers added to its objectives 'to encourage and assist in the preservation of the family' (Holman, 1998). Subsequently, 'the 1963 Children and Young Person's Act for the first time authorized local authorities to spend money, including giving assistance in cash, in order to avoid the need to receive children into care' (Jackson, 2006, p. 15).

During the 1950s and 1960s, the family group home became the main unit for the long-term placement of children and young people, designed to reflect the 'conventional' family as far as possible. However, Frost, Mills and Stein (1999, p. 22) discuss the primary development of this period as being the challenge to the residential institution which came from the research of John Bowlby (1953), whose highly-influential theory of maternal deprivation argued that disturbed or delinquent behaviour by children and young people was the result of lack of consistent and adequate mothering during their early years. Frost *et al.* describe how, as well as being consistent with the official preference for fostering (which, as previously mentioned, was favoured as being closer to a 'normal' upbringing), Bowlby's research 'also coincided with the concern of the social democratic consensus to break with the Poor Law, which was symbolised by institutionalised forms of care' (*ibid.*, p. 22). The official attitude towards residential provision was also reinforced by the findings of research undertaken by Goffman (1961), which was highly critical of the impact of institutions on their inmates.

Sinclair and Gibbs (1998) argue that the basis of the research which fuelled the disapproval of residential care was unsound, given that Goffman's work was heavily influenced by a study of just one psychiatric institution and Bowlby's by a kind of orphanage which England no longer had. Frost, Mills and Stein (1999, p. 22) in summarising the impact of Goffman's and Bowlby's work, noted how it helped 'establish a clear hierarchy of child placement – adoption, fostering and, least desirable, residential care', a hierarchy which has continued to the present day, albeit that the numbers of children placed for adoption have fallen away in recent years.

Jackson (2006) provides an account of how for a time during the 1970s, two events caused the pendulum briefly to swing back towards a policy of intervention. The publication of the book *Children Who Wait* (Rowe and Lambert, 1973), which showed the large number of children drifting in residential care who could have been placed in foster or adoptive families, and the death of Maria Colwell, an eight-year-old girl killed by her stepfather after being returned to the care of her mother (Colwell, 1974), led to the Children Act of 1975. The Act required local authorities to become adoption agencies, outlawed private adoption placements, made it easier to dispense with parental consent and gave greater security to long-term foster placements. In addition, 'the rising care population during the 1970s was also driven by the idea that attending to the welfare needs of children would diminish their propensity for crime, with the result that "delinquent" children were drawn into the child welfare system' (Hannon, Wood and Bazalgette, 2010, p. 53). The 1969 Children and Young Persons Act introduced an ethos of treating youth offending and sometimes non-attendance at school as a child welfare issue and the courts made many care orders under section 7(7) of that Act.

Nevertheless, the 1975 Act was only implemented in part and, 'had much less impact on the lives of children in care than its advocates had hoped' (Jackson, 2006, p. 17). However, it is clear that children in the late 1970s and early 1980s had a significantly higher chance of being in public care than at any time since.

The care population today

In response to the ideological swing against interventionism, the number of children in care as a whole has fallen significantly over the past 30 years, from 92,000 in 1981 to 54,000 in 1998 (Fawcett, Featherstone and Goddard, 2004, p. 76), through to 67,050 as at 31 March 2012 (Department for Education, 2012). In Wales the figure is 5,726; in Northern Ireland it is 2,644 and the latest statistics for Scotland reveal a figure of 16,171 (BAAF, 2012 www.baaf.org.uk, Welsh Assembly Government, 2012; Scottish Government 2012). Overall, the main reason why social care services first engaged with children who were looked after during the year ending 31 March 2012 in England was because of abuse or neglect (62 per cent). However, Table 2:1 highlights considerable overlap with the child protection system and provides a comprehensive overview of the English care population at the time of writing. Seventy-eight per cent of children and young people in care were white. Fifty-five per cent were male and 45 per cent female, with 56 per cent aged over 10. In addition, statistics (DfE, 2012) reveal that 75 per cent of children and young people were in a foster placement, showing an increase from 69 per cent in 2006. Approximately nine per cent were in some kind of residential provision, although this statistic encompasses placements ranging from residential children's homes, through to secure units and hostels. 2,680 were placed for adoption.

Children and young people's experiences of the care system in the United Kingdom can vary according to area. Indeed, the Care Matters working group on the future of the care population concluded that, 'the care system might more realistically be viewed as being not one but 150 different systems'. For example, Narey (2007) found that there were 13 children per 10,000 of population in care in Rutland, compared with 221 per 10,000 of population in the City of London. Such variations cannot entirely be explained by local socio-economic disadvantage. Variation also extends to the type of placements that local authorities opt to provide, with the proportion of the care population in residential care varying significantly between local authorities (from 4–28 per cent). Deloitte (2007) found that London and the North West place 24 per cent and 17 per cent respectively of the total number of children and young people in residential care, while five regions each place ten per cent or fewer of the total number of children in residential care.

Children and young people can become looked after under the auspices of a compulsory care order under section 31 of the 1989 Children Act, where they have suffered or been at risk of suffering likely 'significant harm' attributable to the care given or likely to be given. Here, the local authority assumes parental responsibility, shared with the birth parents. 'Harm' here may include being considered at risk of involvement in criminal activity. Although it is no longer possible to make a care order on the grounds of criminal proceedings, individuals may be placed on a care order if they are considered to be 'beyond parental control'. Young people can also be voluntarily accommodated under section 20 of the Act. Here their parents continue to have parental responsibility and, in theory at least, should play a major role while their children are accommodated. In the year ending 31 March 2011, 60 per cent of children were the subject of Care Orders. Thirty-one per cent were voluntarily accommodated under section 20 and seven per cent were taken into care on some other basis (child protection orders, freed for adoption; Harker, 2012).

In a further example of how policy, practice and the nature of the care population can change in response to reported scandals, Macleod *et al.* (2010) showed clear evidence to indicate that levels of section 31 applications made by English local authorities rose in the wake of publicising of the case of Baby Peter (in November 2008), and in the period that followed continued to rise to a level higher than any experienced since April 2007. The case known as 'Baby P' saw a 17-month-old, Peter Connelly, die after suffering sustained abuse despite being on Haringey Council's at-risk child protection register. In the aftermath there was an increase of 13 per cent from 2,008 to 2,012 of the number of children and young people in care. In addition, the Legal Aid Sentencing and Punishment of Offenders Act 2012 now stipulates that all young people remanded in custody must be recognised by local authorities under the umbrella of children and young people in care.

Hannon, Wood and Bazalgette, (2010, p. 58) discuss how the care careers and placements of children and young people tend to vary with their age at entry, and with behavioural and family characteristics. Their research revealed how a number of young people who had entered care at a young age enjoyed stable placements for over a decade, while others who had entered later moved in and out of care numerous times without ever finding stability. They describe how Sinclair *et al.* (2007) undertook a major study of the movements of children in and out of the care system in 13 councils. On the basis of their findings they identified several distinct 'groups':

- *Young entrants (43 per cent of the sample).* These children were under the age of 11 and were looked after primarily for reasons of abuse and neglect; 29 per cent of them had returned home at least once (and so were counted as a 'repeat admission').
- *Adolescent graduates (26 per cent).* These young people were first admitted under the age of 11 but were now older than this and still looked after. They had generally entered for reasons of abuse or neglect. 56 per cent of this group had returned home at least once.
- *Abused adolescents (9 per cent).* This group was first admitted over the age of 11 for reasons of neglect or abuse. They often exhibited challenging behaviour. 44 per cent of this group had returned home at least once.
- *Adolescent entrants (14 per cent).* These young people were first admitted when aged 11 or over when their relationships at home had broken down. They also showed more challenging behaviour and 50 per cent had returned home at least once.
- *Children/young people seeking asylum (5 per cent).* These children were almost always aged over 11 and were doing comparatively well at school, displaying less challenging behaviour. 21 per cent of this group had had at least one repeat admission.
- *Disabled children (3 per cent).* These children had comparatively high levels of challenging behaviour but their families were not said to have problems in their own right. 46 per cent had returned home at least once.

According to Sinclair *et al.* these groups of children and young people differed in their chances of achieving a permanent 'family' placement and in the way they were likely to find it. The young entrants were divided between those who were adopted, those who went home and those who stayed on in the care system. Adolescent graduates and the small group of severely disabled children were largely dependent upon the care system for whatever stability they were going to achieve. Abused adolescents and adolescent entrants could go home or remain in the care system but in either case their chances of achieving a long-term stable family placement were less favourable than those of others. Hannon, Wood and Bazalgette assert that:

> Alongside their age and reason for entering, one of the most important influences on the shape of a child's care journey is what happens to them *'before'* they enter the system'. The majority have a history of abuse and neglect, and the impact of this pre-care adversity will often contribute to the emergence of emotional and behavioural difficulties later on. (2010, p. 59)

Although problems were less common for younger age groups, Sempick *et al.* (2008) found that 72.3 per cent of children in care aged 5–15 in their study showed indications of emotional and behavioural problems on entry into care. With regard to children already in care, Van Bienum (2008) points to research indicating a high prevalence of mental health disorders. He goes on to discuss a study by McCann *et al.* (1996) which found a prevalence rate 67 per cent for psychiatric disorders in teenagers living in residential units and foster care, compared with 15 per cent of adolescents who lived with their own families.

Table 2:1 Children looked after at 31 March 2012 in England by gender, age, category of need, and ethnic origin

	Numbers	*Percentages*
All children looked after at 31 March 2012	67,050	100
Gender		
Male	37,020	55
Female	30,030	45
Age at 31 March (years)		
Under 1	4,190	6
1 to 4	12,430	19
5 to 9	12,700	19
10 to 15	24,150	36
16 and over	13,580	20
Reason for being looked after		
Abuse or neglect	41,790	62
Child's disability	2,280	3
Parents illness or disability	2,680	4
Family in acute stress	6,000	9
Family dysfunction	9,530	14
Socially unacceptable behaviour	1,150	2
Low income	120	–
Absent parenting	3,490	5
Ethnic origin		
White	52,050	78
Mixed	5,960	9
Asian or Asian British	2,820	4
Black or black British	4,510	7
Other ethnic groups	1,290	2
Other (refused or information not yet available)	430	1

Numbers have been rounded to the nearest 10. Percentages have been rounded to the nearest whole number. – = Negligible (percentage below 0.5 per cent).

Source: Department for Education, 2012

Meltzer *et al.* (2003), found that 49 per cent of 11- to 15-year-old children and young people in care had a psychiatric disorder sufficiently severe to impair their social functioning, compared to 11 per cent of children and young people living in private households. The most common mental health problems in children in care were found to be conduct disorders (around 40 per cent, compared to 5 per cent in children in private households), followed by emotional disorders (12 per cent compared to 6 per cent). In terms of placement type, the highest rates (68 per cent) of mental disorder were found in those who were looked after and accommodated in residential homes. This is relatively unsurprising, given that contemporary residential care continues to be viewed as 'last resort' provision for the most challenging children and young people.

Nevertheless, while there is certainly research evidence to suggest the presence of emotional and behavioural difficulties both among young people at entry to care and those already in care it is entirely possible that *both* pre- and in-care experiences could potentially contribute to such disorders. The turbulent nature of the early lives of many young people has already been alluded to, but certain aspects of life in care, including placement instability and the stresses of living in certain environments, could also precipitate or exacerbate mental health problems. A study by Rubin *et al.* (2007) of children and young people in foster care in the United Sates found that regardless of their characteristics and pre-care experiences, instability significantly increased the probability that they would have behavioural problems. The study suggests that the experience of placement breakdown and instability can exacerbate or even be a cause of emotional and behavioural problems for children and young people in care. As such, it is important not to allow the official focus on the psychology of the individual (historically dominant in social policy initiatives), to enable systemic deficiencies to be ignored or side-lined.

Contemporary policy and practice

The Children Act 1989 and its companion set of Regulations and Guidance was significant in providing the current legal and regulatory framework for care in England and Wales. The Children and Young Persons Act 2008 interpolates or substitutes additional sections, and will be discussed below. Many of the provisions of the Children Act 1989 reflect the obligations contained in the UN Convention on the Rights of the Child, which entered into force in the United Kingdom in 1992. It established the principle that the welfare of the child should be the *paramount* consideration in court proceedings relating to their upbringing and that, in contrast to earlier policy, a court should not make a care order unless it is preferable to making no order. In this way, as reiterated by Berridge and Brodie (1998, p. 15), 'the

Act strongly endorsed the view that children are best looked after within their families'. Indeed, the Children Act 1989 clearly promotes parental responsibility, setting out the principle that while the local authority can seek a court order when compulsory action is in the best interests of the child, the first option must be to work with parents by voluntary arrangement unless to do so would clearly be placing the child at risk of significant harm.

With regard to the impact of the 1989 Children Act on children and young people already in care, Fawcett, Featherstone and Goddard (2004, p. 77) see the representations and complaints procedure (section 26) introduced by the Act Delete as a significant step forward in ensuring the provision of adequate platforms for young people to be heard, and point to the clear emphasis in section 22 of the Act and in the relevant Guidance, on the importance of children in care being consulted by local authorities before decisions are made about them. The UN Convention on the Rights of the Child likewise states that children capable of forming their own views must be assured the right to express those views in all matters affecting them (Article 12).

Nevertheless, it would appear that the right to be consulted does not necessarily equate to a child's or young person's opinion being given precedence when the final decision is made. The fact that subsequent legislation, including the Children and Young Persons Act 2008, has had to reiterate this expectation is evidence there is still a long way to go before such intentions are fully realised in practice. Indeed, a report by the Children's Rights Director (Morgan, 2011) found that only 50 per cent of the 179 children and young people in care who were consulted felt their social worker or caseworker took notice of their wishes and feelings with regard to the decisions made about their care. The reasons for this could relate to enduring perceptions regarding the status of children as potential persons, in need of adult guidance and direction, or attitudes concerning the nature of children in care. Emond (2008, p. 183) suggests that it may be argued that viewing children as having social and legal rights has sparked greater debate and frustration among adults than it has among children – even more so among those working with children in public care. Financial factors are undoubtedly relevant too, as resource constraints may limit the available options. Indeed, in practice, the good intentions of the Children Act 1989 were subject to the resource constraints under which local authorities operate, with, in the aftermath of various scandals, child protection work increasingly dominating children's social services to the detriment of family support and active intervention with children in care.

The subsequent Utting (1997) review coined the phrase 'Quality Protects', which became the Department of Health's flagship programme for improving the lives of children in need. The Quality Protects Programme was launched in 1998 and implemented in 1999, with the aim of transforming the management and delivery of children's social services. The main objectives relevant to children in care were: ensuring secure attachment to appropriate carers, maximising life chances with regard to education, health and social care; enabling care leavers to participate socially and economically in society; promoting the meaningful involvement of users and carers in planning services and tailoring individual packages of care; ensuring effective complaints mechanisms; and the protection of children and young people in regulated services from harm and poor care standards (Fawcett, Featherstone and Goddard, 2004, pp. 78–9).

Other key features of the programme included an enhanced performance measurement and inspection regime and the greater involvement of local councillors in implementing the underlying philosophy of *'corporate parenting'*. This entails a local authority and its partners acting together to give each child in care the same support and guidance that a reasonable parent would give to their own child, providing the child with every opportunity to realise their potential. It appears to be a reiteration of the sentiments expressed in the Children Act 1948 and is again emphasised in the Children and Young Persons Act 2008.

However, as with statements regarding children's rights to participate in decision making, the fact that an aspiration needs continual reiteration would seem to suggest that there are other forces at work which have so far proved impervious to legislative initiatives. Indeed, Taylor (2005, p. 45) highlights how, 'research has identified that those involved in corporate parenting have lower aspirations for, and expectations of, young people in public care, both in terms of achievement and behaviour.' Again, financial factors affecting the provision of public services can also be a barrier to the successful implementation of such goals.

The Care Standards Act 2000 supported the introduction of National Minimum Standards for residential child care provision, which were issued in 2002, and the Children (Leaving Care) Act 2000 extended local authority responsibilities towards former children in care. A new initiative, *Choice Protects*, was launched in March 2002 to improve outcomes for children and young people in care through better placement stability, matching and choice. Thoburn (2008, p. 4) considers that this programme was motivated partly by a recognition that the emphasis on adoption in some local authorities had been achieved at the expense of improving standards and choice in foster and residential placements.

The Green Paper *Every Child Matters* (Department for Education and Skills, 2003) widened the policy focus to all children, and was part of the New Labour Government's wider agenda to combat social exclusion. The Green Paper built on existing plans to strengthen preventive services. *Every Child Matters: The Next Steps* (2004) stated the government's aim for every child, *whatever their background or circumstances* (emphasis added), to make sure children have the support they need to be healthy, stay safe, enjoy and achieve, make a positive contribution and achieve economic wellbeing. It sets an agenda of achieving the goal of making sure organisations involved with providing services to children, from hospitals and schools, to police and voluntary groups, team up in new ways, share information and work together to protect children and young people from harm and help them achieve what they want in life. It is again noticeable that, as with the previously described historical initiatives, policies such as *Every Child Matters* do not attempt to challenge the status quo in terms of changing the social and economic circumstances of children and families. The focus is again on enabling individuals to overcome such adversity, against the odds.

Subsequently, the Children Act 2004 made significant changes to the way that agencies work together. It defined new children's services authorities, stating that they have a duty to promote co-operation between specified 'relevant partners' to achieve the five *Every Child Matters* outcomes. Local authorities were required under that Act to lead an integrated delivery through multi-agency children's trusts and local safeguarding boards; to draw up a single children and young people's plan; to appoint a children's commissioner and director of children's services; and to set up a shared database on children, containing information relevant to their welfare.

Nevertheless, despite the plethora of policy initiatives aimed at improving outcomes for both children and young people care, and children in general, outcomes for children in care remain poor. For example, of those children and young people who were looked after continuously for 12-months at 31 March 2011, only 32 per cent achieved five GCSE's at A*–C grades, compared with 78 per cent of their peers (Harker, 2012). Similarly, of the children looked after continuously for 12 months at 31 March 2011 who were aged ten or over, seven per cent had been convicted or subject to a final warning or reprimand during the year. This compares to two per cent for all children (Harker, 2012). The Children, Schools and Families Select Committee Report on Looked-after children (House of Commons, 2011) reported how, in the long term, those who have been in care are over-represented among teenage parents, drug users and prisoners. Research by Worsley (2006) found that 29 per cent of boys and 44 per cent of girls in custody reported having been in care.

It was in recognition of such outcomes that the New Labour Government's Green Paper *Care Matters* White Paper, published in 2006 (Department for Education and Skills, 2006). Referring to government activity aimed at improving state care in the Foreword to the Green Paper, then Secretary of State for Education and Skills, Alan Johnson MP, stated:

Quite simply it is now clear that this help has not been sufficient. The life chances of all children have been improved but those of children in care have not improved at the same rate. The result is that children in care are now at greater risk of being left behind than was the case a few years ago – the gap has actually grown. (Department for Education and Skills, 2006, p. 3)

However, it should be noted that alternative views to the pervasive negativity regarding outcomes for children and young people in care have been voiced. Stein (2006) argues that the consensus that children in care are failing, and that the system is to blame, is wrong for the majority of the young people who come into care. It is pointed out that most children and young people will spend only a short time in care, thus negating any causal link to future outcomes: the average length of stay for all young people in care is less than 2.5 years. It is also argued that poor outcomes often cannot be separated from negative pre-care experiences. Stein (2006) highlights how research studies carried out at the University of York during the last 25 years show that despite their very poor starting points, some care leavers will successfully 'move on' from care and achieve fulfilment in their personal lives and careers, while a second group will 'survive' quite well, given assistance from skilled leaving-care workers, leaving a third, highly vulnerable group of young people who have a range of complex mental health needs and will require assistance into and during adulthood:

> It is this latter group, representing about 3–5 per cent of the … care population, who have become identified in the public and professional consciousness as typical of all young people in the care system, and who are driving the reform agenda. (Stein, 2006)

In addition, Hannon, Wood and Bazalgette (2010, p. 67) argue that there is, 'a credible body of academic evidence that destabilises the view that care is somehow responsible for *creating* poor outcomes', and provide a summary of relevant research. They highlight how, in 2007, a significant overview of that evidence was commissioned by the Welsh Assembly (Forrester *et al.*, 2007). This overview focused on studies that compared outcomes for children and young people who entered care with those for comparable children who did not, studies that looked at the progress of children and young people in care over time, and studies that compared adults who had been in care with other adults who had experienced adversity or difficulty. While acknowledging important gaps in the research, the authors concluded that:

There was little evidence of the care system having a negative impact on children's welfare. Indeed, the picture suggested the opposite – in the vast majority of studies children's welfare improved. This picture was fairly consistent. The overall pattern leads us to conclude that on the whole care is a positive experience for most children and that it appears to improve or at least not harm their welfare. (Forrester *et al.*, 2007, pp. 29–30)

Similarly, a review (Brodie and Morris, 2009) carried out by the Centre for Excellence and Outcomes in Children and Young People's Services found that, 'for most young people entry to care was considered to have been beneficial for their welfare, including their education'. Cameron *et al.* (2007) sought to compare outcomes among care leavers with a *comparable* peer group. While both care leavers and young people 'in difficulty' were more likely than young people in the general population to have had mental health problems, to be disabled in some way, to have had a pregnancy and to have substance misuse problems, it was concluded that overall, care leavers seemed to be doing better than young people who had not been in care. Care leavers were doing better than young people 'in difficulty' when measuring access to housing, educational participation, being in employment, and self-assessment of their health and wellbeing. Nevertheless, although care does not necessarily have a negative impact and can often improve things for some children, this does not mean that it could not be improved. For example, the potential effects of placement movement have already been alluded to, and the author's research (discussed further in Chapter 4; Shaw, 2010) highlighted how experiences within the care system could exacerbate or precipitate problems for young people. Indeed, while stating that the view of a care system failing young people is too simplistic, Stein (2006) goes on to acknowledge both that, *'care could be better'* and that *'just to "survive" or "struggle" with complex needs is not good enough'*.

An examination of the *Care Matters* programme inspires a sense of déjà vu. It is again asserted that the corporate parents' aspirations for children and young people in care should be exactly the same as any parents' aspirations for their own child and proposes a strengthening of the Inspection regime for children's homes. Also stated is the need to improve care planning by strengthening the role of the Independent Reviewing Officer to ensure that the child's voice is heard when important decisions that affect their future are taken. That paper discusses the need to ensure that young people up to 18 are not forced out of care before they are ready by giving them a greater say over moves to independent living, and the need to provide more personal and financial support for care leavers. Other reforms, which have been incorporated into the Children and Young Persons Act 2008, include a new general duty on local authorities to take steps to ensure sufficient accommodation that is appropriate to the needs of the children and young people they look after within their local authority area, unless that is inconsistent with a child's welfare. In addition, unless it is inconsistent with a child's welfare, local authorities will have to give preference to placing a child with a relative, near their home, and with siblings, if they are also in care. They are also required to ensure that education or training is not disrupted, ensure that every school has a designated teacher for children in care which will promote and encourage their achievement, and ensure those who enter custody are visited regularly by the responsible local authority.

However, while such aspirations are again laudable, it remains to be seen whether, in practice, any real change will occur. For example, given the diminution in local authority residential care provision which has occurred over recent years, and reliance on often out-of-area private provision, it is difficult to see how, within budgetary constraints, councils will be able to fulfil the requirement to provide sufficient accommodation within their areas. Also, stating that a child/young person need not be placed within their local authority area if it is *inconsistent with their welfare*, is a crucial caveat, and undeniably subjective in its interpretation. At the moment, children and young people who are voluntarily accommodated under section 20 of the Children Act 1989 lose their looked-after status when they are sentenced to custody.[1] Therefore, until this loophole is closed, they will continue to lose the entitlements to assistance that looked-after status brings. Indeed, although the new requirement for local authorities to visit children and young people in prison has been extended to those who were voluntarily accommodated immediately before entering custody, it is not explicitly stated that they will have to assess and provide services for them, or arrange for them to have somewhere to live.

Importantly, again these policies continue to focus on organisational and bureaucratic change within children's services, rather than the wider social and economic factors that contribute towards bringing children into care in the first place. In addition, the legislation does nothing to address the culture of managerialism and risk management which has come to dominate social policy and practice and, as will be discussed in relation to residential care (see Chapter 4), has the potential to profoundly impact on the reality of young people's care experiences.

---

1 As it stands, the only children with 'looked-after' status in custody are those under a full care order (s. 31), those children who are classified as 'in need' under section 17 of the Children Act 1989 by the local authority in which the establishment is based during their time in custody, or those 16- or 17-year-olds who have spent enough time in care to be 'relevant' children (The Howard League for Penal Reform, 2009, p. 10).

Specifically with regard to placement type, the *Care Matters* paper (Department for Education and Skills, 2007, p. 57) acknowledged that residential care has an important role to play as part of a range of placement options, but again endorsed foster and kinship care (where children are placed with family members), as the ideal for the majority. The existing hierarchy of placements was thereby retained. However, the Coalition Government elected in 2010 seemed to go a bit further, by agreeing that residential care can make a significant contribution to good quality placement choice for young people, but also by stating that, 'local authorities should see residential care as a positive placement option to meet a child's needs rather than as a last resort where fostering placements break down' (House of Commons, 2011).

Nevertheless, given the cost of residential care placements, it is unlikely that they will come to be a widely used alternative to the other options. Indeed, it is important to note that although the ideological factors described at the beginning of this chapter influenced the retreat from residential care and the move towards family-based alternatives, this trend has also been influenced in part by financial/economic considerations, which make adoption, foster and kinship care more attractive to social service departments endeavouring to balance limited budgets. Smith (2009, p. 7) discusses how the doctrine of managerialism was introduced to the public services in the 1980s by Margaret Thatcher's 'New Right' Conservatives, and that its watchwords were *'the three Es: economy, efficiency and effectiveness'* (*ibid.*, p. 7). In 2010 the average cost per child or young person in care per week in a residential home was £2,689, compared with £676 for foster care (Department for Education, 2011a). When a child is adopted, financial responsibility is assumed by the adoptive parents. Indeed, since coming to power, the Coalition Government has emphasised its eagerness to see an increase in adoption levels after the number of children placed for adoption fell by 15 per cent between March 2009 and 2010. New guidelines drawn up by the government state that older children and young people and those from ethnic minorities should all be considered for adoption by suitable families of any background, regardless of their racial background or social status.

With regard to the provision of care in general, the current Coalition Government has stated that it is, 'convinced that for some children, in some circumstances, care should be seen as the best available option rather than a last resort' (House of Commons, 2011). This is a significant departure from the principle set out in the Children Act 1948 and again re-endorsed in the Children Act 1989, that a care order should only be made if absolutely necessary. In the aftermath of cases such as that of Baby P, there seems to be a greater political will to see public care as a viable and sometimes desirable option. Speaking on 30 September 2010, Children's Minister, Tim Loughton, said that the government wanted to see local authorities working more effectively to place children, 'whether that's in foster care, residential care, or adoption'. The Munro Review of Child Protection (2011) recommended a reduction in bureaucracy in order to better assist professionals in working with young people. However, there is little doubt that financial considerations will again have a part to play and the reality of drawing more young people into the care system at an increased cost to social service departments may mean that such intentions do not become reality.

Conclusion

This chapter has explored the origins of state care provision for children and young people, highlighting how the socio-economic status and perceived nature and characteristics of those who have required assistance, have been particularly influential on policy and practice. Policy continues to be influenced by both ideological and financial considerations, as well as publicised scandals of abuse. This has meant that over time, practice has changed from removing children and young people from their families of origin, often permanently, via a drive to keep families together wherever possible, to a more recent acknowledgement that care might be the best option for some young people. As a consequence, the care population has fluctuated over time, decreasing substantially over the past 30 years. Children and young people now primarily enter care for reasons of abuse or neglect, rather than the financial situation of their families. Financial and ideological imperatives have also influenced the nature of provision on offer; there has been a significant decline in the use of institutional care, in favour of family-based alternatives such as foster care (explored in the next chapter).

This chapter has also reviewed research which has found that the care careers and placements of children vary with their age at entry, behaviour and family characteristics, often influencing the success and stability of placements. Nevertheless, it is also the case that in-care factors, such as placement instability, can contribute to negative outcomes regardless of their characteristics and pre-care experiences.

There has been an exploration of the plethora of policy and practice initiatives which have been introduced over recent years aimed at improving the experiences of those in care. While some outcomes remain poor, Stein (2006) has argued that the consensus that children are failing and that the system is to blame, is wrong for the majority of people who come into care. Indeed, the research reviewed in this chapter has revealed that care leavers do better when compared with comparable peer groups. Nevertheless, there is still a long way to go, and improvements need to be made in order to ensure that the underlying philosophy of 'corporate parenting' is fully realised in practice. This may mean not only ensuring that local authorities have the financial means to implement new policy initiatives, but also that underlying attitudes regarding the nature of children and young people, particularly those in public care, are challenged.

3 Living in foster care

The mainstay of the care system

The best experience of being in care is moving to the foster carers I'm with. I had a fantastic experience because my foster mum took me to India for being so good, because when I was 10 I was told I'd never be any good. I couldn't read and write until I was 12 but I finished up with 11 GCSEs and because of that they took me to India. I loved it. When I was living all over the place I never had holidays unless it was Skegness.

(Chelsea, in care 1990 and 2000s)

For both ideological and financial reasons, foster care has come to be utilised as the placement of choice for the majority of children and young people in care. Being more reflective of the 'conventional' family and considerably less expensive than residential care alternatives, it is popularly thought to facilitate better outcomes for children and young people. As of 31 March 2012 (Department for Education, 2012) 75 per cent of those in care in England were accommodated in a foster placement, which is testament both to its enduring and increasing popularity.

Similarly, in Wales, 77 per cent of young people were accommodated in foster placements (Welsh Assembley Government, 2012) and in Northern Ireland the figure was 74 per cent (BAAF, 2012; www.baaf.org.uk). In Scotland, the latest available figures reveal that 31 per cent were placed in foster care. However, a far higher number of young people (24 per cent) were placed with friends or relatives than in England, Wales and Northern Ireland, and 34 per cent were placed at home with their parents (Scottish Government, 2012). This chapter discusses the current nature of the foster care role, highlights and explores the ever-expanding range of placements available to children and young people, presents a sample of the recent research on foster care, and considers how theory can be utilised to inform practice. It then highlights and evaluates recent policy and practice initiatives, including the proliferation of 'evidence-based' intensive fostering programmes.

Foster care today

Davis (2010, p. 19) notes that there is no single legal definition of fostering, but states that we can infer the following key elements:

- Foster carers look after children who are not their own and for whom they do not have parental responsibility (PR): fostering is all about looking after someone else's children.
- Foster carers care for children who are looked after by local authorities.
- They do so in their own homes as part of a family, not in an institution: there are normally no more than three unrelated fostered children in one home (so that it does not become like a children's home) and carers must agree to look after fostered children as if they were their own.
- It is a temporary arrangement (albeit sometimes long-term) always subject to review, unlike the permanence of adoption.
- The agencies involved, not the court, decide which child is placed with which foster carers.

It should be noted that where children and young people are looked after full time by relatives, family friends or paid 'stranger' carers in private fostering arrangements, they are not regarded as children in care. The local authority is only involved after the arrangement has been made, in order to ensure that it is suitable and to monitor the situation. This chapter primarily concerns approved foster care for children looked after by local authorities.

Ward and Munro (2010) highlight how the principle enshrined in the Children Act 1989 that practitioners and carers should work in partnership with parents has, 'radically altered the nature of the fostering task'. They describe how:

> The Children Act 1989 accelerated an emerging trend away from the perception of foster care as an exclusive, quasi-adoptive arrangement in which birth parents played only a minimal role, towards more inclusive work with birth families, the objective of which is reunification. Foster parents are no longer expected to replace children's parents but to work in partnership with them, facilitating contact and eventual return – a point emphasised by the change in nomenclature to foster carer (Ward and Munro, 2010, p. 138).

This statement makes it clear that foster care has changed enormously over recent years. Being nice people who open up their home to a child in return for an allowance to cover expenses is no longer enough: carers are increasingly recognised as an essential part of the children's workforce, participating in the management of the case, working in partnership with social workers and family placement workers as well as with parents. This change in the nature of the fostering task has been one of the key factors that have led to increased calls for professionalisation of the role. As will be described further at a later point, initiatives have been spearheaded to develop foster care into a professional service with appropriate working conditions, holiday entitlement and adequate levels of remuneration.

Such calls have also been fuelled by the extension of the population for whom fostering is considered a viable option: a number of foster carers recruited to work on specialist schemes have formal qualifications in teaching or psychology and are trained to offer a highly skilled service. Indeed, Whittaker and Cressey (2010, p. 16) note that:

> Foster family care ... has expanded to include a wide range of shared and kinship-care variations along with a variety of purposefully designed intensive treatment interventions using the foster family as an integral platform for service delivery, often as an alternative to residential placement.

This observation reflects how contemporary foster care placements are many and varied, and can include:

- Short-term placements for children and young people removed in emergencies, or for babies who are to be placed for adoption.
- Placements for teenagers with a view to moving them on to independence.
- Respite care for children and young people with disabilities.
- Therapeutic fostering for children and young people with highly challenging behaviour.
- Specialist remand foster placements.
- Long-term fostering for children and young people who are unlikely to be placed for adoption.
- Kinship care placements where a child or young person in care is placed by the local authority with a family member or friend.

Therefore, unlike residential care, which is often used as a last resort placement for generally older, more challenging children and young people, foster care is utilised for children of all ages who have a variety of needs.

Fostering services (which encompass local authority fostering services, independent fostering agencies and voluntary organisations) are governed by the Care Standards Act 2000 and the detail is filled in by the Fostering Services (England) Regulations 2011, which revoked and replaced the

Fostering Services Regulations 2002. In addition, National Minimum Standards (NMS) for Fostering Services (Department for Education, 2011a) were set by the government and are used by Ofsted in their inspections of fostering services. Statutory English official guidance for fostering services, *Children Act 1989 Guidance and Regulations Volume 4: Fostering Services* (Department for Education, 2010c), sets out the wider context for local authorities, as providers and commissioners of fostering services. This is not an exhaustive list, and other legislation and guidance may also be relevant, for example, legislation covering such matters as health and safety, fire or planning requirements.

The *Permanence Study* (Sinclair *et al.*, 2007) revealed that private or voluntary organisation care was mainly provided outside the local authority area, and had the advantages and disadvantages associated with this. The main disadvantages revealed were barriers to family contact, costs of travelling for all parties and difficulties of making educational arrangements outside the area. It was also found that young people might also return home from distant placements to areas where they have lost all ties. Nevertheless, such placements outside the area can be more specialised (having a wider catchment area) and can break undesirable ties to delinquent groups, prostitution and so on. Such provision is often more costly and local authorities used it for specialist placements which they cannot provide themselves. Examples of this included placements for black and minority ethnic children in certain areas for 'difficult' adolescents, and placements which rose as a result of simple lack of provision in others. The study showed large differences between local authorities' use of kin care and care from the independent sector.

Recent research in foster care

Until the mid-1990s most British research in the field of children and young people in care dealt with residential care or the care system in general. However, Sinclair (2010, p. 189) highlights how recently: 'a number of British studies, many sponsored by the UK government, have variously focused on foster carers, fostered adolescents, kin care, contact between foster children and their families and children who were adopted or fostered long-term'. Examples of such research are the *Permanence Study* (Sinclair *et al.*, 2007), and one group of studies, the *Fostering Studies* (Sinclair, Baker, Wilson and Gibbs 2005; Sinclair, Gibbs and Wilson 2004; Sinclair, Wilson and Gibbs 2005). In addition, an earlier selection of 16 studies which focus on similar and related issues is reported upon by Sinclair (2005).

The *Permanence Study* considered difference in outcomes between stranger fostering, fostering with relatives and friends and fostering in private or voluntary agencies. It failed to find any difference in outcomes between foster care provided by the independent and local authority sectors. Sinclair (2010, p. 192) reports that it found that stranger foster carers carried out all fostering roles but that kin carers and those in the independent sector had, to some extent different roles and characteristics. Kin care was predominantly used for children who came into care when relatively young and stayed there for a long time.

The *Fostering Studies* revealed that placements with family and friends were typically seen by social workers as of lower quality than those with strangers. They were, however, more likely to be seen as achieving their purpose, lasted longer than others and the children and young people in them scored better on the studies' measure of wellbeing. The *Permanence Study* showed that kin care in authorities that made frequent use of it did not seem to have worse results. As a consequence, Sinclair (2010, p. 193) advocates that, 'there is therefore a case for increasing its use, thus at once reducing what is seen as a severe shortage of stranger carers and freeing those carers for roles other than long-term care'.

While research has found that foster care can provide long-term, stable care in which children and young people remain in contact with their foster family into adulthood, for most young people this is not the reality of their experience. A pervasive and enduring concern about the care system is its instability, and high rates of foster placement breakdown have been reported amongst older children and young people, particularly those aged 11–15. In this age group studies have suggested a rate of around 40 per cent in the first year and around 50 per cent with longer follow-up (Sinclair, 2005, p. 30).

Sinclair (2010, p. 194) reports that the *Fostering Studies* found that in general, placements that tended to go well seemed to have similar characteristics to those that did not break down. He notes that they were alike in:

- *The children and young peoples' characteristics*: children were more likely to stay and do well in their placements if at 14 or 36 months earlier they wanted to be fostered and did not have serious problems in their behaviour and their ability to relate to others.
- *The carers' characteristics*: carers who at 14 or 36 months earlier were rated by the social workers as seeing things from the child's viewpoint and as caring, accepting, encouraging, and clear in their expectations and not easily upset by the child's failure to respond were more likely to have successful, lasting placements. So too were those who scored high on a self-completed test of 'child orientation'.
- *The 'fit' with the foster family*: children and young people who at 14 or 36 months earlier were accepted by the main carer and other children in

the family (if any) and the other foster children (if any) were much more likely to have successful, lasting placements.

- *Family contact*: children and young people who had previously been abused and who had 'unrestricted' access to their current families were three times more likely to have breakdowns.
- *Schooling*: children and young people who were described by their carers at 14 or 36 months earlier as 'enjoying school' were much more likely at follow-up to be doing well and much less likely to have had a breakdown.
- *Services*: children and young people who had contact with an educational psychologist were more likely to avoid breakdowns.

Therefore, overall, a number of factors have been found to be predictive of the success or failure of placements, including 'carer characteristics', 'child/young person characteristics', their experience of school, nature of contact with home and the 'fit' or 'chemistry' between a child/young person and a particular foster home. In general terms, it was not found that success varied with the age of carers and numbers and ages of other children in the placement, the presence of siblings in the placements or number of previous placements (as opposed to disruptions). However, such variables *can* be important in particular cases and as such, the findings 'suggest a need to listen carefully to what both foster families and children/young people want and to avoid 'rules of thumb' (Sinclair, 2010, p. 195).

The *Permanence Study* built on and reinforced some of the findings of the *Fostering Studies*. It showed that children and young people were more likely to move from placements intended to last if they were older, had 'challenging behaviour' and did not want to be in care. Children and young people were likely to be given higher ratings for 'wellbeing' if their carer was rated by another social worker as warm, clear in expectations, and so on. However, carer characteristics only had an impact on stability if the young person was over 11 and the placement was meant to last. Some younger children stayed in placements where they were acutely unhappy perhaps because they were unable to voice their dissatisfaction.

The combined research also revealed that the success of a particular foster placement does not necessarily lead to long-term success. Indeed, it was found that some problems are intractable, and others that are resolved in placement may recur when a child or young person moves to a new environment. Sinclair (2010) suggests that poor assessment prior to discharge can contribute to this. For example if children and young people are returned or moved on to unsuitable environments, then chances are that progress may be undone. Poorly managed transitions can also be a factor, such as where children are not enabled to stay in touch with previous carers to whom they have formed attachments.

In terms of how the results of such research could inform policy, Sinclair (2010, p. 203) highlights how certain broad recommendations flow from the findings:

- More use should be made of kin placements by those authorities that make use of them, but care needs to be taken over their difficulties (poverty, quarrels between kin and so on).
- Much more attention needs to be paid to the problem of producing high-quality placements: initially through quality assurance schemes and later through the development of effective selection, training and support.
- Similar attention needs to be paid to the problems around contact with parents, schooling and the 'poor fit' between some children/young people and otherwise high-quality placements.
- Much more attention needs to be paid to the transition between successful placements and subsequent adoptive placements, return home and independent living.

Gender and race in foster care

Sinclair (2005) reports that while gender has not been found to be associated with placement outcome, it is however, an issue to which foster carers give importance and can therefore impact upon the experiences of children and young people. Some express strong preferences for taking males or females. Some carers are anxious about allegations of sexual abuse and avoid leaving male carers alone with female foster children. One study found that foster carers were significantly less sensitive to the needs and anxieties of adolescent girls than boys (Farmer, Moyers and Lipscombe, 2004).

Although much is often made of the desirability of matching children and young people with carers from the same ethnic background, Sinclair, Gibbs and Wilson (2004) and Thoburn *et al.* (2000) found that ethnic minority children/young people placed with carers from ethnic minorities were no more or less likely to have a placement breakdown than similar children/young people placed with a white British family. In addition, Thoburn *et al.* (2000) found that boys from minority ethnic groups were less likely to experience placement breakdown when placed with white families than with parents of similar ethnic background, whereas with girls the reverse was the case. Sinclair (2005, p. 73) reports that, 'despite these rather ambiguous results Thoburn *et al.* (2000) do not conclude that minority ethnic children and young people could be as well placed with white families as not'. He explains that they and other researchers argue that:

- Qualitative data make clear the importance of ethnicity to the black and Asian children/young people and extra difficulties that white carers have in bringing them up.
- Minority ethnic children and young people have to make sense of their histories as foster children/young people from particular ethnic groups. Depending on their circumstances and opportunities for contact with family and other black people they variously worked at these issues or 'put them on the back-burner' awaiting a time when they could turn to them.
- Matching may well need to take account of more subtle characteristics than simply whether child/young person and carer are both from minority ethnic groups. In individual cases other considerations such as religion may be very important.
- Such refined matching may be difficult because, e.g., the proportion of minority ethnic carers from a particular group may be very small and the chance that they have a vacancy at the time when a particular child or young person from their group has a need may well be very low.
- This would suggest that relative carers may have a particular advantage for this group but the proportion of relative carers from ethnic minorities was not, in the core studies, higher than it was among the 'ordinary' foster carers.

A comprehensive discussion of the issues of race and gender in foster care is beyond the scope of this chapter. However, ethnicity in relation to adoption is considered in Chapter 5. However, the question of whether more time and resources should be devoted to finding suitable carers from a wide variety of backgrounds is clearly an important one, as is the issue of how gender can impact upon the experiences of children and young people and the steps that can be taken to reduce any potentially negative outcomes.

What young people say

The thoughts and feelings of children and young people who have had experience of foster care are both revelatory in terms of illuminating the 'reality' of foster care and clearly vitally important to any consideration of future policy directions. Sinclair (2005, pp. 50–51) reports that research has found that children have five different requirements:

- *Normality*: Children and young people want fostering to be as normal as possible. They do not like having to delay decisions about going on school trips or 'sleepovers' to be put off while permission is sought from a social worker. They do not like to be embarrassed at school because reviews are held there about them or because their method of getting to school (e.g. by taxi) singles them out.

- *Family care*: Children and young people want to feel that they belong in their foster home, that they are treated the same as other children in the home and ideally, that they are loved, listened to and encouraged. They resent harsh or inconsistent discipline, and any feeling that their foster carers are 'just doing it for the money'. They value treats, opportunities for their hobbies and, in most cases, a room of their own.
- *Respect for their origins*: Children and young people do not want a conflict of loyalty between their foster carer and their family. They have differing views about how far they want to belong to their own family or to their foster family and about which members of their family they wish to see. They want those views respected.
- *Control*: Fostered children and young people want their views to be heard and seriously considered. They differ in their requirements for a placement. Some want to be with other children/young people, some like houses in which there are babies, some want to be with their siblings and so on. They differ in how happy they are in their placements, in the relationship they would like to see between their placement and home, in the members of their family they want to see, in the frequency with which they want to see social workers and much more besides. They dislike situations where it is not clear what plans have been made for them or where they are moved suddenly and with little notice. They want social workers to be aware of their feelings on these matters and to take action accordingly.
- *Opportunity*: There is no evidence that fostered children and young people differ from others in what they want for their futures. Success at school, a good job, a happy family and children are all common aspirations. Nevertheless, there is some evidence that in some respects their aspirations are limited. The safest assumption is that they want foster care to be a springboard for getting their lives in order and on track for what most of us would regard as success. Carers were praised for not only providing a family environment and making the children and young people feel valued but also for offering opportunities and enabling skills.

Such requirements as voiced by children and young people reveal a system which, while having its good points, is also in need of improvement at various levels. Indeed, overall, a number of areas for change and improvement have been identified as a result of the research discussed in this section. In recent years successive governments seem to have been listening. Policy developments and practice initiatives are described in the final section of this chapter.

Theory in foster care

A number of theories have been utilised in the study of foster care. Among those are attachment theory, theories of the consequence of maltreatment, and theories relating to the proper way to parent. The application of such theories has and continues to inform practice with children and young people. Indeed, John Bowlby's (1953) seminal theory of maternal deprivation, which argued that disturbed or delinquent behaviour from children and young people was the result of the lack of consistent and adequate mothering during their early years, was a key factor in the move away from residential care to foster care. The idea that secure attachments in childhood can promote positive outcomes amongst children and young people continues to be highly influential, with foster care and adoption being popularly viewed as the ideal means to facilitate such relationships.

'Resilience theory' is highlighted by Sinclair (2005, p. 51) as being probably the most general of the theories used, which 'essentially… is a list of 'protective factors' thought to increase the chance of good outcomes among children otherwise at risk of poor ones' [outcomes]. Although different writers produce different lists, three protective factors have been shown to be particularly associated with better outcomes for all young people, as we discuss further in Chapter 8 (Daniel, 2008, p. 62):

- at least one secure attachment relationship
- access to wider supports such as extended family and friends
- positive school and/ or community experiences.

Such goals seem achievable for foster care, being both relevant to the children's difficulties and in line with what the children want. Indeed, Daniel (2008, p. 67) highlights how, if the aim of intervention with children and young people in care is to nurture resilience, five strategies have been identified:

1. Reduce vulnerability and risk

For example, Daniel (2008) argues that when young people engage in risky behaviour it can indicate that they lack a sense of future and purpose. As a result of this, the focus of work with them should be on developing a sense of hope, thereby encouraging them towards a position where they want to protect themselves from risky situations and where they see themselves as having some choices of direction. This is in line with the young people's stated desire for opportunity and success.

2. Reduce the number of stressors and 'pile-up'

Young people in care are often bombarded with a number of stressful events at once. For example, a move to a new foster placement might also entail the loss of previous attachments and connections, a move to a new school and so on. When assessing and planning in foster care placements, it is therefore important to look at ways that potential stresses can be staggered.

3. Increase the available resources

Foster carers can provide valuable human resources for young people and the potential for these relationships to engender positive outcomes should not be underestimated. Daniel (2008) highlights how there is evidence that young people can learn new patterns of attachment from positive relationships. It is stated that through the opportunity to experience different types of relationships with adults, young people can experience:

- trust
- having their views listened to
- being given choices
- being appreciated for their individuality
- the chance to talk over their options, and
- support.

(Daniel, 2008, p. 69)

In addition, carers can work with young people to identify other people in the formal and informal network who can offer support and act as a bridge to facilitate and/or re-establish contact.

4. Mobilise protective processes

Focused intervention by a skilled foster carer could help a young person to improve their ability to appraise situations which might otherwise cause them difficulty and choose appropriate strategies to deal with them. Such interventions could certainly be part of the everyday fostering practice and in newer initiatives, such as multidimensional treatment foster care, there is particular focus on the development of appropriate social and reasoning skills.

5 Foster resilience strings (where improvement in one domain has a positive knock-on effect in other domains)

There are a number of domains of a young person's life where intervention can be targeted, including:

- secure base
- education
- friendships
- talents and interests
- positive values
- social competencies.

(Daniel and Wassell, 2002a and 2002b)

Daniel (2008) describes how in fostering resilience strings, the aim is for improvement in one domain to have a positive spin-off in another. A study (Daniel and Wassell, 2005, p. 18) which examined the value of assessing these domains in children and young people living in foster care suggested that they helped enhance the knowledge of the child and self-knowledge by the child, thus reinforcing the positives.

Therefore, in the context of foster care, resilience theory suggests that working on improving such areas could be of enormous benefit to the young people and produce positive outcomes.

In addition, Sinclair (2005) argues that other less general theories are also relevant to foster care:

> Theories of parenting are relevant to the tasks foster carers undertake. These theories generally emphasise the need for parents to combine support with control or guidance. In line with this, social workers look to placements to provide adolescents with stability, nurture and clear guidance. Older foster children want to be valued by their carers and dislike approaches to discipline that they perceive as harsh, unreasonable or unfair. Foster parents may need to be particularly skilled if they are to provide appropriate discipline without making their foster children feel rejected. (2005, p. 52)

Theories of identity are also relevant to the tasks faced by foster children who have to come to terms with their relationship with their birth family, their anomalous situation in someone else's family and perhaps their ethnicity:

> The studies provide plenty of evidence that foster children are concerned with these issues. They resent attempts to interfere with their view of

their family relationships. They value carers who support their view of their own ethnicity' (Sinclair, 2005, p. 52).

Overall, therefore, it is clear that theory has helped to illuminate that 'a reasonably comprehensive list of the key needs of foster children would therefore include':

- 'good enough' parenting (nurture and 'boundaries'), probably informed by insights from social learning and attachment theory
- the development of good attachments
- good education and experiences of school
- support for children in developing their sense of identity – particularly as this refers to their relationship with their family, their experience as a foster child, their ethnicity and their general view of themselves, and
- support for friendships and the development of skills and interests. (Sinclair, 2005, p. 52)

Evidence-based programmes

In recent years a number of evidence-based programmes aimed at providing interventions for children and young people who are deemed to be most challenging both on the 'edge of care' and when in care, have gained political support. Here we focus primarily on one such programme, the MTFC (Multidimensional Treatment Foster Care) programme, as an example both of the ever-expanding role of foster care and its increased specialisation. It is also an example of the application of theory to practice, for example in terms of the mobilisation of protective processes through the development of appropriate social and reasoning skills, the promotion of attachments and positive school experiences, and the application of parenting which combines support with control or guidance.

Multidimensional Treatment Foster Care (MTFC)

MTFC was originally developed and evaluated in the US in the 1980s as a cost-effective alternative to residential treatment for adolescents with complex needs and challenging behaviour, including offending behaviour. Children and young people chosen to participate would usually have very challenging behavioural problems and have experienced multiple placement breakdowns. They are sent to live with specially-trained foster parents who are supported 24 hours a day by a team of health, education and social care professionals. Individual treatment programmes are created for each child/young person. Each set of foster parents looks after just one child/young person for between six months and a year, concentrating on behaviour management to promote emotional stability and the skills needed to live in a family. The specialist foster carers are supported on a daily basis by a team which usually includes:

- a clinical psychologist who develops the intervention programme for each child/young person
- skills coaches who assist the child/young person in social activities
- an education worker who provides guidance to the child/young person's school, teachers and mentors
- a family therapist who works with the birth family to ensure the placement is supported by contact and helps prepare the follow-on family.

The foster carers themselves benefit from:

- specialist training in the MTFC model
- a clear detailed behavioural programme designed for each child/young person which is developed by the programme supervisor: taking some of the stress off the foster parent
- weekly carers' support group
- respite care from other MTFC carers
- 24/7 on-call support from the MTFC team
- a substantial financial remuneration package.

The programme is based on teaching children and young people new skills – in their foster home, school and social environments. The focus is on supporting and encouraging positive behaviour and setting clear and consistent limits. Keeping children and young people away from peers who are a bad influence is also central.

Funding for MTFC was initially granted by the former Department for Children, Schools and Families (DCSF) in 2002, a commitment continued by the Department for Education (DfE). A total of 18 local authorities in England piloted MTFC in the form of three different programmes for children and young people of different ages.

- The 'adolescents programme' for young people aged 11-16 designed to help them make the most of relationships with friends and family, to get on well in school and to enjoy leisure activities.
- The 'children programme' for 7-11-year-olds aimed at helping them develop skills in relationships, improve behaviour and get on well in school.
- A third programme – 'prevention' – aimed at averting children aged 3–6 from the risk of developing behavioural difficulties and helping them learn to thrive in a classroom environment.

Biehal *et al.* (2012) investigated whether placement in MTFC results in improved outcomes, relative to the usual care placements, and which children are most likely to benefit from it. The Care Placements Evaluation (CaPE) studied 219 young people (including 63 per cent of those placed nationally in the MTFC project between October 2005 and December 2009). This is only the second independent study of MTFC and the first to evaluate its use with older children in the care system in the UK.

For the sample as a whole, placement in MTFC showed no statistically significant benefit over the usual care placements. This was true for all the outcomes studied including overall social adjustment, education outcomes and offending. However, in a subgroup of the sample with serious antisocial behaviour problems, MTFC showed improved reduction in these behaviour problems over usual care and also in overall social adjustment. Nevertheless, the young people who were not anti-social did significantly better if they received a usual care placement.

In addition, earlier research by Biehal, Ellison and Sinclair (2011) highlighted the counter-productive effects of poorly managed transitions from the programme. They report the results of an independent evaluation of the MTFC programme for young offenders in England. In this study, young people sentenced to MTFC were compared to a similar group, matched on the eligibility criteria for MTFC, the majority of who were sentenced to custody. The groups were well matched in terms of their characteristics and criminal histories.

At the one year point after their entry to MTFC or release from custody, the MTFC group were less likely to be reconvicted, had committed fewer and less serious recorded offences, on average, and took longer to commit their first recorded offence. At this point the MTFC group were more likely to be living with their families and less likely to be in custody than the comparison group. However, at that one year after exit stage no significant differences in patterns of reconviction remained. It was therefore concluded that MTFC successfully contained a high-risk group in the community, but the effects of the intervention washed out once they left their foster placements. It was thought that environmental effects on entry to and exit from the MTFC placements might help explain the results at both stages.

Nevertheless, The Coalition Government's response to the report of the Children, Schools and Families Select Committee (2011), stated that such programmes, 'if implemented with model fidelity, clinical supervision and support, have been shown to improve outcomes, provide better value for money and result in fewer placement breakdowns'. The government has therefore committed (via the Department for Education business plan) to roll out evidence-based intensive fostering interventions (including MTFC and Keeping Foster and Kinship Carers Safe and Supported (KEEP) which is a less intensive version of the training component of MTFC) in 20 new local partnerships. The Department will work with sector partners and early implementers to draw on the learning from the initial pilot programmes to test out new commissioning and delivery models and develop the market for these programmes. The stated aim is to move towards a fully sector-owned programme during the course of the Spending Review period. However, the research conducted so far has revealed less than encouraging outcomes and, it is also clear that much closer attention needs to be paid to what happens to children and young people when they leave such programmes and how any successful results can be maintained.

Policy and practice developments

In terms of further recent policy and practice developments in the field of foster care, the *Care Matters* White Paper (2007, p. 57) endorsed foster and kinship care as the ideal for the majority. This policy statement advocated improving foster care by setting clear standards outlining the skills that all foster carers should have and increasing access to specialist training and support. The White Paper stated that:

> Foster carers are central to many children and young people's experience of care. It is essential that we value and support them and ensure that they are properly equipped with the necessary range of skills. (pp. 8–9)

Proposals included amending the National Minimum Standards in foster and residential care; ensuring better enforcement of these standards to improve the quality of provision for children and young people in care; and preventing local authorities from discharging young people prematurely from their care placements until they are properly prepared and ready to move on to the next stage of their lives. The intention was to pilot ways to enable young people to remain with foster carers up to the age of 21, providing greater stability for young people more in line with that of their peers. Consequently, the previous UK New Labour Government set up the 'Staying Put' (known as 'Right2BCared4') pilot to assess the benefits of allowing children and young people to stay in care and with foster carers past the age of 18. The £4.5 million pilot scheme, which started in October 2007, and ran until March 2011, enabled young people in 11 local authority areas of England to stay with their foster families until they turned 21. The pilot councils used the funding to recruit project-specific workers, provide training and advice to young people and pay carers. The evaluation concluded as follows:

There has been a cultural shift in professional attitudes concerning care planning and decision-making for young people aged 18 and over ... a higher proportion of those [young people] in the pilot authorities were looked after until they reached legal adulthood compared to those from comparator authorities (Munro *et al.*, 2011, p. 1)

The UK Coalition Government, elected in 2010 introduced a wide-ranging programme of reform with the stated aim of improving the entire care system, by making sure that all children in care have greater stability, less upheaval and a better chance at a stable family life. It launched a Foster Carers' Charter in March 2011 (DfE, 2011) which was jointly produced by government, fostering organisations, charities and children. At the time, Children's Minister Tim Loughton said:

Foster carers are the unsung heroes of our care system. They do a fantastic, selfless job helping often vulnerable children build stable relationships that can endure into adulthood. Too often I hear stories about foster parents feeling isolated, unsupported, and facing endless red tape when all they are trying to do is enjoy everyday activities with their foster child – like taking them on holiday or even for a haircut. The new Charter will help to change that. It underlines the huge value we place on foster carers. Not only as role models to the children who look up to them, but also as pushy parents who put those children first. The Charter sets out clear principles of what support should be available and what foster carers can expect.

There is little doubt for doubt about the importance accorded to fostering in the care system in that statement. Tim Loughton wrote to Directors of Children's Services on 27 August 2010 to emphasise that foster carers 'should have the maximum appropriate flexibility in taking decisions about children in their care'. The government has stated its determination to remove what the Children, Schools and Families Select Committee (2011) called the 'highly bureaucratic and risk-averse culture' which can put off potential carers and impede some foster carers from providing the children they care for with the love and support they need. Indeed, a stated aim of the Charter is to encourage more people to sign up to be foster carers.

The Charter states that children and young people in foster care deserve to experience as full a family life as possible as part of a loving foster family, with carers who can make everyday decisions as they would their own child and without the child feeling that they 'stand out' as a child in care. This is certainly a reflection of the research findings reported in this chapter, where the young people stated their need for 'normality' and 'family care'. Such research findings are also reflected in the emphasis placed by the Charter on children being given every support to develop their own identities and aspirations, fulfil their potential, and take advantage of all opportunities to promote their talents and skills, and its position that 'above all, they should be listened to'.

It is stated that local authorities and fostering services must:

- Recognise in practice the importance of the child's relationship with his or her foster family as one that can make the biggest difference in the child's life and which can endure into adulthood.
- Listen to, involve foster carers and their foster children in decision-making and planning, and provide foster carers and their foster children with full information about each other.
- In making placements be clear about the continuing care or support to be provided (including for the child into adulthood); be sensitive to the needs of the foster carer and the child/young person in making and ending placements; and have contingency plans should the placement not work.
- Treat foster carers with openness, fairness and respect as a core members of the team around the child/young person and support them in making reasonable and appropriate decisions on behalf of their foster child.
- Ensure that foster carers have the support services and development opportunities they need in order to provide their foster child with the best possible care. That includes liaising with local foster carer groups and seeking to respond to problems and disseminate best practice.
- Make sure foster carers are recompensed on time and are given clear information about any support, allowances, fees, and holidays they will receive, including where there are cases of dispute with the service or gaps in placements.

Such aspirations are further evidence of the recognition increasingly being accorded to foster carers as an essential part of the children's workforce, participating in the management of the case. They are also evidence of the increased professionalisation of the role, with an emphasis placed on the need for appropriate working conditions, holiday entitlement and adequate levels of remuneration. It is also stated that foster carers must:

- Provide positive adult role models, treat the foster child as they would their own child, and be a 'pushy parent' in being an advocate for all aspects of the child's development, including educational attainment and physical and emotional health and wellbeing, and co-operating fully as part of a team with other key professionals in the child's life.

• Support their foster child and do all they can to make the placement work. Take part in learning and development, use skills and approaches that make a positive impact and enable the child to reach his or her potential. Support their foster child to help them to counter possible bullying and discrimination as a result of their care status.

While it is not compulsory for local authorities and fostering agencies to sign up to the Charter, Children's minister Tim Loughton stated that he particularly wanted local areas to 'sign up to the spirit of the Charter' and 'build on and develop it in their own way to reflect the needs of the local community'. The Charter is backed up by the new slimmed-down fostering regulations and guidance which came into force April 2011, the stated aim of which is to make clear to fostering services what their statutory duties are, and reduce burdens placed on them.

However, while there is little doubt that such aspirations are laudable, it is also the case that, as discussed in greater detail in Chapter 2, history has shown that despite continual reiteration certain ideals fail to be met. For example, from the Children Act 1948 onwards, emphasis has been placed at various points on the need for children to be provided with every opportunity to realise their potential. Similarly, the Children Act 1989 emphasised the importance of listening to the views of children and young people, an ideal which was reiterated in the Children and Young Persons Act 2008. However, for a multitude of reasons, including the ingrained attitudes of those responsible for children and young people in care, such aspirations fail to be met. Indeed, history has also shown that in practice the good intentions of many an initiative aimed at improving the care system have been stymied by the resource constraints under which local authorities operate and the pressures faced by social workers when attempting to manage the requirements of a large case-load. In times of severe cuts to public sector provision, and the current high vacancy rate for social workers in England and Wales, it will remain to be seen whether the stated aims of the Charter can indeed be fulfilled.

A further area of policy development worthy of mention is the stated aim of the UK government to improve the placement of children with family and friends. In recognition of the fact that the Children Act 1989 puts local authorities under a duty to consider placing children and young people in care with family and friends carers unless this would not be reasonably practical or consistent with the child's welfare, the government has issued revised statutory guidance on family and friends care (DfE, 2010). The guidance came into force on 1 April 2011 and its stated aim is to help ensure that children and young people who are living with relatives or friends receive the support that they and their carers need to safeguard and promote their welfare.

The guidance explains the current legal framework as it relates to family and friends care. It provides guidance to local authorities in relation to the delivery of effective services to children and young people living with relatives in informal arrangements or with relatives or friends who are approved as local authority foster carers, or who hold a residence order or special guardianship order in relation to the child/young person. It is stated that:

- A range of agencies providing family support and early intervention services should be aware of and sensitive to the needs of children who are living with family and friends carers and children and their families should receive good quality services which meet the needs of every child.
- To enable family and friends to offer appropriate care for children and young people who cannot live with their parents, access to a range of high-quality support services at universal, targeted and specialist levels will be needed.
- Local authorities and their partners should make sure that family and friends carers are aware of relevant support services, and that these can be readily accessed by those caring for children whether or not these are looked after by the local authority.
- It is essential that services are not allocated solely on the basis of the child's legal status, and that commissioners and services providers are aware that many children in family and friends care have experienced multiple adversities similar to those of children who are looked after by local authorities.
- Where support services are identified as necessary to meet the child's needs, these should not be withheld merely because the child is living with a carer under an informal arrangement rather than in a placement with a foster carer or with a person with a residence or special guardianship order or an adopter.

Here we have clear evidence of the recognition by the UK government that family placements can be an invaluable means of providing care and support to children and young people who are otherwise unable to live with their birth parents – as seen in Scotland. In addition, the emphasis placed on services being available to children and young people living with carers in an informal arrangement is perhaps an acknowledgement of the substantial savings that can be made when a child or young person is not officially received into care.

Conclusion

This chapter has provided an overview of the current nature of the foster care role, highlighting the ever-expanding range of placements available to children and young people. It has discussed how the nature of the fostering task has radically altered in recent years, with carers now being expected to work in partnership with birth families, facilitating contact and eventual return. They are seen as an essential part of the children's workforce, participating in the management of the case. Foster care is also now seen as a platform for the delivery of intensive 'evidence-based' intervention programmes with children and young people who are deemed to display particularly challenging behaviour. As a consequence of such developments, there have been increasing moves towards the professionalisation of the role of foster carer.

We saw the potential of theory to inform practice in foster care, particularly in relation to the impact of resilience theory in facilitating improved outcomes for children and young people. Multidimensional Treatment Foster Care was discussed as an example of the application of theory to practice, as well as the ever-expanding role of foster care and its increased specialisation.

Foster care has been the subject of much recent research and a number of subsequent policy and practice initiatives have been introduced by the current UK Coalition Government and previous New Labour administration with the stated aims of improving the situation of both children and young people and foster carers. It will remain to be seen whether such initiatives achieve the desired outcomes. We now move on to explore the provision of residential care for children and young people.

4   Living in a children's home

Empowerment or institutionalisation?

> The kids home in Manchester, the manager she was alright. She treated all the kids as her own and I still go to see her.
>
> (Zac, in care 1990s and 2000s)

There is little doubt that the small percentage of children and young people who currently live in children's homes in England and Wales face issues and challenges that are particular both to the residential environment and the workings of the care system within which they are looked after. Such issues and challenges involve a number of factors, including the impact of individual experiences prior to entering care, the dynamic of the particular resident group, how staff interact with the young people and the operation of individual children's homes, the response of social services professionals and care home staff to challenging behaviour, and the overall status of the residential care sector. The race and gender of the young people are also pertinent factors.

The following chapter begins by providing an overview of the current residual residential care sector in the United Kingdom. It then explores the two macro theoretical perspectives of Goffman (1961) and Foucault (1977) in relation to how they could explain the behaviour of young people and professionals in the institutional context. The impact of inquiries into abuse in residential care is critically examined, with consideration of how the subsequent regulation of the sector has influenced attitudes and practice. There then follows a discussion of life in residential care, including how the group dynamics of individual homes, their ethos and approach to young people, staff–resident relationships, responses to challenging behaviour, and race and gender can influence experiences and outcomes for the children and young people. Recommendations for policy and practice are made along the way. Finally, we summarise current policy developments and possible future directions.

Residential care for children and young people today

In the year ending 31 March 2012, approximately nine per cent of young people in care lived in some kind of residential provision in England (DfE, 2012). Although this statistic encompasses placements ranging from residential children's homes through to secure units and hostels, the focus of this chapter will be on residential children's homes in their various contemporary forms. Statistics for Scotland and Northern Ireland are identical at nine per cent, with Wales achieving approximately five per cent (Scottish Government 2012; BAAF, 2012; www.baaf.org.uk; Welsh Assembly Government, 2012). In response to the ideological concerns and financial factors described in Chapter 2, the use of residential care in the United Kingdom declined substantially throughout the 1980s and beyond, the proportion having decreased steadily from 40 per cent in the mid-1970s (Health Committee: 1997–8). Petrie *et al.* (2006) point out that the percentage of young people in residential care in the United Kingdom is low by comparison with other European Union countries: in Denmark and Germany over half of young people in care are in residential placements, in The Netherlands just under half, and in France just over a third. This highlights how such provision is viewed in a more positive light in other jurisdictions and is consequently accorded higher status and greater financial resources. The 'last resort' status of residential children's homes in the United Kingdom has been perpetuated still further by the scandals of abuse which came to light in the 1990s. At this time, residential homes are mainly used as provision for older young people, disabled young people, and those considered as having severe problems, making them unsuitable for fostering.

The proportion of the care population in residential provision varies significantly between local authorities (from 4–28 per cent: DCSF, 2008), and councils adopt differing policies on the place of residential care in their care system. Unlike in other policy areas, such as health and community care, where the independent sector is financially incentivised over public provision, there has not been a deliberate strategy of promoting and prioritising 'independent' children's units. However, the retrenchment in residential care and subsequent reduction of 'in-house' local authority homes has nevertheless provided fertile ground for a burgeoning private sector. A 2009 report for the National Care Association, 'Every Budget Matters', revealed that 60 per cent of children's homes in England were within the private sector. Such units are located throughout the country and are often willing to accommodate young people from any local authority area. This can result in young people being placed at a considerable distance from family and friends. Indeed, in 2010, 2,300 (47 per cent) of the children and young people placed in regulated children's homes were placed outside their local authority area. On average, local authorities placed 55 per cent of their children and young people in other areas, with 22 placing *all* outside the local authority area (Department for Education, 2011). Such practice also demonstrates that although the removal of young people from their home areas, as advocated by the 'child rescue' ideology of the past (see Chapter 2), might have been officially renounced, market forces have precipitated similar effects.

In relation to nursing care, which is further along the road than children's services in terms of privatisation, Scourfield (2007, p. 70, cited in Smith, 2009) concludes that, 'business values, reductions in costs and income generation have become prioritized above the quality of care'. However, in the context of their study of residential care homes, Berridge and Brodie (1998) found that the homes that scored highest in terms of quality of care came from different categories, covering both public and private homes. Indeed, there was more variation *within* categories of home than between them. Nevertheless, given the increase in private residential units over the last ten years, the question of whether placement type might impact on quality of care seems as pertinent as ever.

The retrenchment of local authority provision has also gone hand-in-hand with the move towards perceiving ever smaller units as desirable in terms of their ability to achieve better outcomes, as advocated by Sinclair and Gibbs (1998). Consequently, many larger local authority units have been closed and replaced by smaller homes, with the subsequent shortfall in provision being made up largely by the private sector. Units housing six to eight young people appear to be commonplace, although it is not unusual, especially in the private sector, for them to provide a home for fewer young people, even just two or three.

Clough, Bullock and Ward (2006, p. 61) point out that the issue of the optimal size of a residential home is key. They find that there are widely divergent views on the size of home, and that while Sinclair and Gibbs' (1998) study leads to a clear statement that on the whole, it is better to keep the size of children's homes small, Chipenda-Dansokho *et al.* (2003) claim that theirs is the only major study providing evidence in support of smaller units. Indeed, Clough, Bullock and Ward (2006) go on to argue that:

> Very small residential homes are extremely costly to staff and seem to emulate some of the characteristics of a foster home without the key factors that make a foster home akin to a family setting: the fact that foster parents share the home with the child and do not go on and off duty. In small homes each child has far greater potential to disrupt the stability of life in the residential home, and produce a situation in which much of what happens is a direct response to his or her own behaviour. (2006, p. 61)

They point out further that a small home denies the potential for young people to be supportive to others in groups. Indeed, the author's own research (Shaw, 2010) found that for many children and young people in residential care, peer associations become an important source of empowerment and self-worth, and that to be isolated from other young people cut them off from a valuable source of social capital and made them feel estranged from 'normal' life. Of course, this must be balanced against findings regarding the potential for negative peer cultures, bullying and violence in the residential context (to be discussed below).

Theoretical approaches to residential care

A number of theoretical approaches have been applied to residential care at both macro and micro level. Macro theories attempt to provide overarching explanatory frameworks, and micro (often behavioural) theories, claim a relevance to direct practice with children and young people. A comprehensive exploration of these theories is beyond the scope of this chapter. However, here we discuss two macro theoretical perspectives in relation to how they could explain the behaviour of young people and professionals in the institutional context, thereby shaping the experiences of residents.

Goffman utilises a symbolic interactionist perspective, which, as originated by George Herbert Mead, sees 'the self' as a social construct, and the way in which individuals act and regard themselves as being, in part, a consequence of the way others see and react to them. Goffman's study of one psychiatric hospital, published as *Asylums* (1961), examines how institutions work, and may therefore help in the understanding of how and why the exercise of power in such contexts can impact on residents' behaviour. Goffman utilises the concept of the 'total institution'; those institutions which encompass the three key aspects of our life–work, play and sleep. While most people undertake these activities in different settings, for residents of total institutions, all these activities take place in the same site and under the same form of authority. He argues that these institutions are, 'forcing houses for changing persons; each is a natural experiment on what can be done to the self' (1961, p. 22). Goffman asserts that from the moment a person enters such an institution, they are required to accede to its authority, which involves what he identifies as a 'degradation ceremony'. This takes place at the moment of admission to the institution, when a resident/inmate arrives carrying with them the signs and symbols of their own unique identity: clothes, hairstyle, jewellery. In order for the resident to be integrated into the total institution they must be stripped of the signs of this identity. Residents or inmates may adopt a number of strategies in order to cope with the regime, along a continuum which ranges from taking on board the values of the institution, to blatant resistance (an idea similar to that expressed by Michel Foucault, see below), and the institution, in turn, operates in accordance with a system of 'punishments and privilege' (1961, p. 53), whereby it reacts to cooperativeness (or lack thereof) in order to maintain its authority.

Many contemporary residential children's homes do not now operate along the lines of a 'total institution', with schooling and leisure activities often (although not invariably) taking place 'off site' and with many units being much smaller than in previous years. Nevertheless, Goffman's ideas may still be applicable to children's experiences of residential childcare, and inform our understanding of the effects that living in such places may potentially have on the behaviour of residents. Indeed, when children and young people arrive at a residential unit from their previous environments (whether their family home, foster care or another residential placement), although they may not be required to change their hairstyle or surrender jewellery, they are still required to 'fit in' and comply with the rules, regulations, expectations and ethos of the home. They may be required to get up at a particular time in the morning, eat meals at certain times, request permission to undertake activities that they would usually take for granted, attend school and comply with a curfew, all of which may be contrary to and conflict with, their prior experiences and consequent identities, values and sense of 'self'. They may then adopt various tactics in order to cope with the regime, which might include challenging it. Indeed, the research undertaken by Kilpatrick, *et al.* (2008) would seem to be evidence of this: namely the argument that a trigger of challenging and disruptive behaviour was the institutionalised nature of some homes and associated rigid rules and regulations. Clough (2000) quotes from Parker's summary of research, that different regimes have a differential effect on children's behaviour and that 'the best results are achieved by child-oriented rather than institution-oriented practices' (Parker, 1988, p. 111). Therefore, the exercise of power within the homes is potentially an extremely important area for further exploration and has the potential to impact significantly on outcomes for young people.

Indeed, Layder highlights how in intimate, primary or private spheres of life (e.g., personal or intimate relationships) there is greater latitude for appropriate or tolerated behaviour:

> In these more 'liberal' settings, people are freer to interpret behavioural requirements whereas in more formal and restrictive settings … closer conformity to 'established' practices is required (2004, pp. 16–17).

It is certainly the case that in residential environments, children and young people are the subject of increased regulation, with staff being required to adhere to the overarching requirements of legislation, rules and regulations, as well as practices which may vary from home to home. While a degree of regulation may benefit young people who have previously lacked structure and guidance in their lives, it may also result in conflicts with young people who have very often been unused to such control, surveillance and scrutiny in their home circumstances.

Michel Foucault's theories relating to disciplinary power in the context of social institutions are also of particular relevance. Frost, Mills and Stein (1999) discuss how, the idea that social institutions are constructed as part of the exercise of power which governs even the most private aspects of our lives is at the centre of Foucault's thought: they are the 'material expressions of the exercise of this power'.

Foucault (1977) writes of the creation of an obedient subject, through the imposition of habits, rules and orders. In contrast to theories, such as those advocated under the umbrella of individual positivism which place the human subject as the origin of meaning, he views the individual as, 'a container whose self-identity and psychological interior is largely a product of the relations of power, discourse and practice in which he or she is enmeshed' (Layder, 2006, p. 126). In order to achieve disciplinary power in the context of social institutions such as the residential children's home, the techniques of hierarchical observation, normalising judgement and examination, are utilised. Hierarchical observation constitutes a constant surveillance, the principle of which, although external in origin, eventually becomes internalised and self-regulating, while at the same time, 'there is pressure upon the individual to conform to some standard of "normality" whilst within the domain of surveillance' (Layder, 2006, p. 122). The individual's own self-regulation is again absorbed as part of the general system of surveillance, which is exemplified by the use of dossiers, marking and classification systems (and other forms of appraisal and monitoring (or examination). Disciplinary power is imposed not only at the level of the individual children's homes, but also by the external disciplinary (or social control) mechanisms of the wider care system. Certainly, life in contemporary children's homes is one of surveillance, with the activities of residents monitored through the keeping of copious records relating to their everyday movements and activities, as well as their overall progress. While resident in such placements they are required to act in accordance with prescribed standards of normality, which for a number of children and young people may have positive benefits. For example, a 2009 Ofsted report (Morgan, 2009) found that some young people felt that the fact that staff made sure they got up on time and went to school or did homework had helped them to do well with their education.

Nevertheless, Foucault also asserts that where there is power, there is resistance. Therefore, although certain official standards of 'normality' may be imposed within the domain of children's homes, which are in turn usually in accordance with the dominant discourses of wider society (relating, e.g. to conceptions of childhood, gender roles, and so forth), the children and young people within the homes may behave in ways which are consistent with previously imposed standards of normality, emanating from their family, peer group, or community. This is congruent with Foucault's assertion that, 'power is everywhere … it is not simply the province of privileged or "legitimate" authorities' (Layder, 2006, p. 130). These previous standards of normality may be in conflict with the dominant values of the children's home (and society), thus precipitating 'deviant' or 'challenging' behaviour. Contemporary residential care is seen as very much last resort provision for the most challenging children and young people. However, such theories provide an insight into how life in children's homes could potentially shape the responses of their residents and also prove challenging for young people who must adjust to the requirements of (sometimes numerous) regimes.

Abuse in residential care

Among the experiences endured by young people in residential care has been that of physical, sexual and emotional abuse in various forms. Indeed, it is indisputable that residential care, more than any other form of state care, has become synonymous in recent times with the idea of child abuse. However, Smith notes that:

> Aside from the various inquiries, the actual evidence of widespread abuse in care settings is not strong. It would appear to be no more likely in residential than in foster care (Kendrick, 1998) or in community settings where adults have access to children (Gallagher, 2000) (2009, p. 42)

Certainly, foster and kinship care placements have had their share of scandals, the highest-profile in recent years being the murder in 2000 of Victoria Climbie by her guardians. Publicity surrounding the death of Peter Connelly, after having suffered sustained abuse from his mother and her boyfriend in November 2008 provides a further example of abuse within a 'family' setting. Nevertheless, the perceived link between residential care and child abuse has been both pervasive and enduring and has contributed to the 'last resort' status of the sector.

Smith (*ibid.*, p. 35) summarises the literature in identifying three categories of institutional abuse:

- *overt or direct abuse* perpetrated by an individual adult on a child
- *programme abuse* where theoretical models are misapplied, and

• *system abuse* where deficits in the wider child care system prevent children from reaching their potential.

Stein (2006) adds *organised abuse* as a further category and notes that in many cases categories overlap. A number of residential child abuse scandals came to light in the 1990s, which were investigated in a series of inquiries and reports.

The first of the major inquiries into residential care concerned the 'Pindown' regime which operated in two children's homes in Staffordshire in the English Midlands between 1983 and 1989. 'Pindown' was a crude, 'behaviorist' regime which operated a number of variants along a continuum of severity. Young people were controlled through isolating them and depriving them of a range of rights and liberties. During the time it was in operation, 132 children, some as young as nine years old, experienced Pindown, some for weeks at a time. 'Unlike other abuse scandals there [were] no attempts to conceal the details of the Pindown regime – the logbooks detailing the restrictions of liberty were freely available and the regime had the explicit approval of senior managers in the social work department' (Smith, 2009, p. 39).

In response to emerging concerns about the state of residential childcare, highlighted by the Pindown experience, the UK government commissioned Sir William Utting to conduct a general review of the sector in England and Wales, published as *Children in the Public Care* (1991). This made a range of recommendations around staff selection and training and called for improved procedures. Similarly, *Another Kind of Home* (Skinner, 1992) set out a number of principles, providing a general framework for residential child care practice in Scotland.

The Warner Report (1992) *Choosing with Care,* was commissioned in the wake of the notorious case of Frank Beck, who presided over a regime of physical and sexual abuse under the guise of 'regression therapy' in children's homes in Leicestershire between 1973 and 1986. *Choosing with Care* concluded that recruitment practices in residential child care were unsatisfactory, with the employment of workers who had no suitable qualifications or experience commonplace. Smith argues that, 'this led to a tightening of methods of selection leading among other things to the increasing use of police checks and more systematic recruitment processes' (2009, p. 40).

In response to further reports of abuse which were mainly historical in the sense of looking at events in the past, the UK government again commissioned Sir William Utting to review the safeguards for children introduced in the 1989 Children Act and to recommend whether these were sufficient and properly enforced. The Utting Report, *People Like Us,* was published in 1997 and the Quality Protects initiative discussed in Chapter 2 stemmed from its many recommendations.

The most extensive inquiry to date into abuse in residential care was led by Sir Ronald Waterhouse and published in 2000 as *Lost in Care*. Waterhouse concluded that there had been widespread abuse in children's homes in the North Wales area and made 72 recommendations. From those emerged the establishment of an independent children's commissioner for Wales and improved procedures for whistle-blowing and for dealing with complaints. Waterhouse also recommended an independent regulatory body to inspect childcare services.

The impact of such inquiries has resulted in ever greater external scrutiny and regulation of the residential care sector. In addition to the inspection of premises against national care standards, there have also been developments to regulate the social care workforce through codes of practice. However, there is little evidence that such developments have actually led to improvement in the sector or to better outcomes for those placed there. In 1998 Berridge and Brodie (1998, p. 10) pointed out that, 'despite various efforts, residential care has continued to be seen as the poor relation of social work. It has lower status and its workforce is less well professionally equipped'. Almost a decade later, Colton and Roberts (2007) make similar observations when they highlight that, 'heavy workloads, poor pay ... and poor supervision impact on turnover rates on both sides of the Atlantic'. Far from being a positive choice for young people, residential care has continued to be seen as a residual service of last resort.

In addition, McLaughlin (2007) argues that regulation is predicated on meta-narratives of abuse, lack of trust and an assumption that social workers require external surveillance to prevent them from abusing those they work with. Smith argues that such mistrust can result in defensive, back-covering practice with children and young people, where the primary task of caring for children becomes subsumed beneath a concern to ensure their own safety:

> Caregivers need to feel safe if they in turn are to value the children in their care. Paradoxically, the more confident and empowered adults feel, the better they are able to listen to and respect children and take their views into account (2009, p. 47)

Such defensive practice can be found in the tendency of residential care staff to involve the police for minor incidents of assault and criminal damage which take place in the residential context, which will be explored later in this chapter.

Rather than focusing on increased regulation, it would perhaps be more useful to consider how perceptions of and attitudes towards young people in residential care can precipitate abuse in the first place. Indeed, Fawcett, Featherstone and Goddard (2004) argue that sufficient recognition of the extent to which prevailing conceptions of childhood, and in particular, looked-after children, was often missing from the debate that emerged about how to respond to this problem and compounded the vulnerability of young people to abuse. They state that:

> Perceptions of looked after children in particular, as either victims (of parental abuse and neglect) or villains (as youth offenders in either practice or training) did not encourage much stress on their agency, subjectivity or rights to participation in everyday decision-making (2004, p. 77).

Certainly, such perceptions would impact on how a young person is treated within residential care and the reactions of professionals when allegations of abuse are made. It is also the case that while not so widely publicised, system abuses, where deficits in the wider child care system prevent children from reaching their potential, exacerbate existing problems or precipitate new ones, can be every bit as damaging. Such deficits arguably include multiple placement movement, or the lack of provision tailored to the needs of individual young people engendered by the retrenchment of the residential care sector. Indeed rather than using the terrible experiences of some young people to justify a continued focus on greater regulation of the sector, it would arguably be of greater to value to pay closer attention to how perceptions of looked-after children and the workings of the wider care system might negatively affect their experiences.

Life in children's homes: the potential for success?

In contrast to the prominence which has been given to accounts of abuse and poor practice in residential care, relatively little attention has been given to those who have reflected positively on their experiences. While not wishing to deny or play-down negative accounts – indeed, this chapter provides abundant detail of such experiences – it is worth noting that research studies have shown that children and young people are more likely to choose residential care over foster care (Sinclair and Gibbs, 1998). Indeed, for some young people who have had negative experiences of family life, or who retain strong loyalties to their families of origin, residential care may well constitute the most attractive option. *Celebrating Success*, part of the review of children and young people in care in Scotland, focused on what helps young people in care succeed:

We met a number of participants who had experienced feeling accepted, secure and a sense of belonging in residential care. In the best experiences, participants thought of their residential carers as a kind of family…What often characterised the positive relationships in residential care was the continuing sense of security and safety, which could be relied upon (Happer, McCreadie and Aldgate, 2006, p. 17, cited in Kendrick, 2008).

Positive accounts of life in residential care were also evident in the 2009 Ofsted report (Morgan, 2009) which found that for some young people, the quality of relationships with children's home staff came out clearly as the main thing that could make living in a home a good experience, followed by available activities, friendships, being 'helped and looked after well', and the facilities in the home. Some described how life had been better for them in children's homes than back at home with their families. Emond (2003) pointed to a number of potentially positive aspects of peer group relationships in residential care; it was found that support was provided in a number of ways, ranging from material provision to advice. In addition, the view that being fostered is generally a more positive experience than living in residential care is not supported by a 2010 report by the National Care Leavers' Association (Duncalf, 2010), with almost one-third more of the 310 care leavers surveyed reporting a 'mainly positive' experience of being in residential care compared to foster care. In his Foreword to the report, Will McMahon, Chair of the National Care Leavers' Association, states that,

This is somewhat at odds with the last two decades of policy, which has witnessed the closure of many residential settings; perhaps the idea that a secure base for those in care can only be created by mimicry of the nuclear family is misplaced, given that for some it was the nuclear family setting that was the original place of harm (McMahon, quoted in Duncalf, 2010, p. 5).

Therefore, despite negative perceptions of residential care, it appears that for a number of children and young people, it will be the placement of first choice and for a proportion of others, one in which they find themselves after the breakdown of other options. Indeed, research evidence has shown that care can be of benefit to young people if they are in placements matched to their needs, including residential care (Forrester *et al.*, 2009). It is therefore imperative that serious consideration is given to what existing research can tell us about both the positive and negative aspects of life in residential care and consequently how the quality of such provision can be improved.

The residential environment

Given the 'last resort' status of children's residential care, it is hardly surprising that the young people who live in children's homes might have a number of pre-existing problems and issues, which could potentially affect their behaviour and subsequent experiences. Indeed, by the time most young people enter a children's home, they will in all probability have experienced some form of abuse and/or neglect in their family of origin, and a number of failed foster placements. Many will also experience multiple failed residential placements. Nevertheless, Sinclair and Gibbs (1998) found that the background features of the children who participated in their research into residential care, did not explain the wide variations in outcomes such as offending behaviour and absconding). Indeed, in relation to such behaviour, their findings suggest that in certain respects, this was very much a creation of the immediate environment. Research has highlighted how the quality of placements are strongly related to children and young people 'doing well' in care, with residential care units that are small, well-managed, with a low staff turnover, a consistent regime and a positive culture producing the best results (for example, see Sinclair *et al.*, 2007). Linked to this, it has been suggested that residential units which have the right 'feel', thus creating a sound basis for therapeutic intervention, are capable of producing positive results (Stevens and Furnival, 2008). Nevertheless, while research has found some excellent examples of practice, the reality for many young people is that they will experience a number of placements of varying quality. The following section will therefore focus on some of the issues facing young people in children's homes and explore how the residential environment might impact both positively and negatively on their behaviour and subsequent outcomes.

Young people and crime in residential care

Residential children's homes have long been recognised as a potentially 'criminogenic' environment (Hayden, 2010) and in the postscript to his report on the abuse of children in care in Gwynedd and Clwyd, Waterhouse concluded that, 'some children … were introduced to delinquency and to harsh regimes in which they were treated by some staff as "little criminals" … some regimes encouraged abscondion and increased offending' (Waterhouse, 2000, p. 840). A summary of research findings published by The Adolescent and Children's Trust (Tact) in 2008, stated that, 'residential care was highlighted in both the literature and in the practitioner survey as the care setting which posed by far the greatest risk to young people in terms of criminalisation' (p. 2) and Sinclair and Gibbs (1998) found that 40 per cent of young people with no cautions or convictions prior to entering care had one after six months or more of living in a children's home.

There has been relatively little research into the reasons for such outcomes. However, a PhD study by the author (Shaw, 2010) found that a range of individual, institutional and systemic factors could contribute, and, citing one of the few recent studies to have focused specifically on the process of criminalisation in residential care concludes that:

> Contemporary residential care (particularly for older teenagers) can present a mutually reinforcing set of risks. These include the mix of residents in some homes, young people going missing overnight, being out of full-time and mainstream education, as well as the distress and disruption associated with the care experience. (Hayden, 2010, p. 471)

Focusing specifically on causative factors within the residential environment, the issue of subcultures within the homes has been highlighted in previous research. Stewart *et al.* (1994, p. 84) found that residential care was frequently, 'a readymade community within which crime was condoned by a subculture of delinquent peers onhand day and night to reinforce social norms'. Taylor states that:

> The 'university of crime' concept may be applicable to certain residential care units, particularly in explaining how residents pick up criminal 'skills' regardless of whether they have previously been in trouble or not. (Taylor, 2005, p. 88)

The question of how relationships with other residents within the context of children's homes could potentially contribute to challenging/offending behaviour is therefore certainly an area worth considering when placing potentially vulnerable children and young people. Indeed, while such relationships can be a source of much needed support (Emond, 2003), they can also precipitate less desirable outcomes.

Peer relations in residential care

Sinclair and Gibbs (1998) found that residents were not happier if they said they got on well with staff or if they reported that they had had a lot of help from the home. Rather, it was the resident group and how they got on with them that seemed to make the difference. In some ways, this is understandable, given that staff operate on a shift basis, whereas the resident group are a more constant presence. Shaw (2010) also found that such attitudes related to previous experiences where, as a consequence of abuse and neglect within the family, the peer group came to replace immediate relatives and adult influence, in terms of providing emotional support and a sense of self worth and status. This often resulted in solidarity between residents against staff or newcomers to a unit. The research also suggested a degree of self-preservation in their actions, where, as is often the case in a prison regime, the young people did not want to be seen as being complicit with the system against fellow residents.

Therefore, it is entirely possible that the young people might develop loyalties to the resident group, in opposition to staff, who could be viewed as part of the 'establishment' and enforcers of the system. This aligns with Foucault's assertion that where there is power, there is also resistance. Other forms of resistance have been documented in residential contexts. For example, Frost, Mills and Stein (1999) report that one of the authors had witnessed a unit where the young people developed an entire secret language which had the effect of excluding staff from their interactions.

Nevertheless, Shaw (2010) also found that some residents felt that they had no choice other than to display solidarity, as they did not wish to be targeted for retribution if they told staff about misdemeanours or criminal activity. Certainly, although solidarity might be displayed against staff, and there is little doubt that relationships with peers can provide a valuable source of support and empowerment, relationships with fellow residents in children's homes can also at times be precarious.

Although abuse by staff in children's homes has received a great deal of attention, 'much of the available evidence has indicated that residents are most often at risk from other young people in the home' (Barter, 2008). Kilpatrick *et al.* (2008) found that the hierarchies of peer groups and the negotiating of position within the group were ever-present sources of disruptive behaviour or peer violence in the residential context. With regard to incidents of low-level physical violence reported in their research, Barter *et al.* (2004) found that boys used this form of violence to publicly present a particular kind of 'macho' or 'hard' masculinity to their male peers. Barter (2008) reports that peer violence has been consistently highlighted by young people in residential care as one of their overriding concerns, and goes on to provide a summary of relevant research. She discusses research from Morris and Wheatley (1994), who found behaviour ranging from teasing or being picked on, to physical attacks, and goes on to describe how Utting (1997) describes the fact that, 'possibly half the total of abuse reported in institutions is peer abuse'. Research conducted by Wade *et al.* (1998) indicates the extent to which running away is related to unhappiness with peers, while Sinclair and Gibbs (1998) report that nearly half (44 per cent) of the 223 young people interviewed stated that they had been bullied during their stay at the homes. Building on her own research (Barter *et al.* 2004), Barter

(2008) reports that four different forms of peer violence were derived from the young people's accounts, including direct physical assault, physical 'non-contact' attacks, verbal abuse and unwelcome sexual behaviours. In the author's research (Shaw, 2010) young people described how the police frequently become involved as the result of conflicts with fellow residents in the homes.

The Ofsted report detailing young people's experiences of life in children's homes (Morgan, 2009), stated that many of the children questioned described having to live with people they did not get on with as one of the worst things about living in a children's home. This could result in a greater potential for friction between the young people and consequent police involvement. Some of the professionals interviewed in the author's research (Shaw, 2010) felt that the emergence of smaller homes had resulted in a reduction of such problems. However, whatever the numbers, there is still the potential for conflict, albeit on a smaller, and maybe more manageable, scale.

However, it should also be noted that the same Ofsted report found that support and help from young people, getting to know young people from different backgrounds and having other children and young people to share interests and activities with were important to many and considered to be some of the best things about living in a children's home. Therefore, it should be borne in mind that the experiences of the young people may differ between placements or that they may experience both positive and negative interactions within the same placement. However, there is little doubt that peer relations within the residential context have the potential to impact significantly on the overall wellbeing of young people and as such, the potential impact of group dynamics should be an important consideration both when placing children and young people, and attempting to understand their behaviour.

Behaviour management in children's homes

Taylor (2005) found that there was general consensus amongst the young people in her research that there was very little that staff could do to control residents (who were usually well aware of that fact). Similarly, Kilpatrick *et al.* (2008) commented that an issue of concern reported frequently by managers and staff in residential care is that of 'keeping order' – of dealing appropriately with disruptive and challenging situations that arise within children's homes. These concerns are also reflected in the comments made by many of the professionals interviewed during the course the author's research (Shaw, 2010), a number of whom felt that the inability of staff and homes to control their residents was a major precipitating factor in offending, and that the children and young people now had too much power in those circumstances. There is no doubt that as a result of such perceptions, members of staff often consider it necessary to resort to official intervention in order to deal with incidents within the residential context.

Fitzpatrick (2009) draws attention to the routine prosecution of minor offences in some children's homes, stating that, 'one inevitable consequence of this is that looked after children can be unnecessarily criminalised for behaviour that is highly unlikely to result in an official intervention for those living at home with their parents'. There appears to be a particularly low threshold reported by some care leavers for police involvement. Research commissioned by the Department of Health (Nacro 2003, 2005) also identified this as a problem, as did Morgan (2007).

In the current environment the use of formal protocols developed by local authorities in consultation with various agencies, including the police, Youth Offending Services and the Crown Prosecution Service appear to be increasing in popularity. Such protocols have the aim of managing behaviour within children's homes, while avoiding recourse to the criminal justice system wherever possible, often through the use of restorative justice techniques. However, police involvement for minor matters remains a persistent problem, which suggests the presence of more deeply ingrained factors, relating to perceptions of young people in residential care and/or the need to maintain the authority of the residential institution and the system, along with a shortage of high-quality staff training. It is also undoubtedly a consequence of defensive, 'back-covering' practice with children and young people, precipitated by increased regulation, and resulting in staff no longer feeling confident enough to deal with matters inhouse.

The author's research (Shaw, 2010) revealed an increasing tendency for children's homes to encourage a routine police presence. Accounts of the local community constable or police and community support officers coming for dinner or calling in for a coffee on a regular basis were commonplace and welcomed by staff. To a certain extent, there seems to be some positive aspects of such contact, including a greater understanding by the police of the young people (something which was commented on by the police officers interviewed) and possible encouragement of staff by the police to deal with matters 'inhouse'. The potential to open up further lines of communication with the young people regarding matters of concern to them was also a possibility. A primary aim of the police service youth strategy, 'It's Never Too Early … It's Never Too Late' (Carter, 2007), which was implemented in January 2008, is to build and maintain positive relationships between all young people and the police. The strategy document states that positive engagement with the police and their local communities will help to identify and support those children and young people who are at risk, and help all children and young people to enjoy a positive role within their communities. It is also stated that the police should aim to take a lead in identifying and diverting those children and young people at greatest risk of becoming involved in anti-social behaviour or criminality, before they enter the criminal justice system and before they are socially excluded. Such aims are in accordance with the *Every Child Matters* objectives described in Chapter 2. Various schemes which encourage police contact with children and young people in residential care have been put in place throughout the country, and seem to be increasing in popularity. However, a question remains regarding whether a routine police presence in the homes of the children and young people should ever be acceptable. Such a presence says a great deal about official attitudes regarding the nature and characteristics of children's homes residents.

A further theme which emerged in the author's research (Shaw, 2010) was that when a young person presents challenging behaviour, she or he is often moved to a different placement. This was an occurrence described by a number of the young people, and at a professional and policy level is an example of the pervasive practice of 'risk management' which, 'has generally involved the re-definition of political, economic and social issues as problems to be managed rather than necessarily resolved' (Muncie, 2000, p. 29).

Often, unless they present particular risks to themselves or others, the young people are initially accommodated in foster care or a local authority residential placement, depending on perceived needs or risks. However, if their behaviour continues to be considered challenging or 'risky', they are then moved on to a succession of (usually private sector) placements in various parts of the country. Clough, Bullock and Ward argue that:

> 'A child doing badly in residential care needs a good-quality intervention, not transfer to another … home. System neglect, whereby the needs of children remain unmet, is less obvious than physical or sexual abuse but is no less dangerous (2006, p. 44)

While the children and young people may be moved on for a number of reasons, some of which are entirely appropriate, it seems inevitable that constant displacement will incur negative effects including a sense of disorientation, fear of further rejection, low self-esteem and an inability to form and maintain close friendships and relationships. Certainly, the notion of young people sabotaging placements through fear of forming attachments and then being rejected again after so many moves was mentioned by some of the professionals (Shaw, 2010), and has disturbing implications for their future emotional and social health and wellbeing. Consequently, very careful thought should be given to whether placement movement is truly appropriate and might cause further harm.

The impact of staff–resident relationships

The question of how children's home staff can contribute to positive outcomes is important. Sinclair and Gibbs (1998, p. 7) reported that links were found between the characteristics and attitudes of the staff and the reactions of the residents, suggesting that staff–resident relationships can both prevent and precipitate challenging behaviour. Certainly, research such as that undertaken by Whitaker, Archer and Hicks (1998), Clough (2000) and Berridge (2002) emphasises that results in children's homes are best where children are accorded respect as individuals and effective relationships built between staff and young people, which take into account the children's perspectives. Berridge (2002) sets out factors that his research suggests characterise good, productive relationships. The most effective staff in this respect are informal in approach, easy to talk to, respect young people, listen to what they say, try to understand and not lecture them and are frank and sometimes challenging, rather than 'pushy' and 'nagging'. Kilpatrick *et al.* also note that the dominant theme running through their study is the fundamental importance of the relationship between the staff and the young people:

> Young people we encountered endorsed the findings from the research review in identifying skilled staff as those who know young people and can therefore anticipate difficult situations, are calm and consistent, can successfully de-escalate situations … listen to young people, take an interest in them … and refrain from playing power games or constantly engaging in verbal battles with them (Kilpatrick *et al.*, 2008, p. 16)

The relationship between the quality of staff–resident relationships and outcomes for young people has been discussed in other research. Taylor (2005) describes how, when talking about why they got into trouble in residential care, many participants in her study spoke of feeling that that they did not have anyone who cared, an issue pertaining to relationships between the young people and residential home staff and associated lack of staff continuity within the homes. To this end, she explains how the social control theory of delinquency developed by Hirschi (1969) sees the delinquent as a person relatively free of intimate attachments, aspirations and moral beliefs that bind most people to a life within the law. Therefore, if criminality is to be prevented, strong attachments should be encouraged and nurtured. That many of the young people, already adrift from their families, might not find such attachments from the care experience is a cause for concern, and, as a consequence, Taylor (2005) suggests that the promotion of attachments in the care context could assist in the prevention of offending and by implication, other challenging behaviour.

Therapeutic approaches: the way forward?

Given the challenging nature of the problems presented and experienced by many young people who enter residential children's homes, Stevens and Furnivall (2008, p. 196) argue that it is 'perhaps an indictment on the state of residential childcare that there are only some types of residential provision which are specifically therapeutic in terms of their practice'. Nevertheless, they go on to highlight how since the mid-1990s, there has been renewed interest in therapeutic approaches to residential care, and argue that a diverse range of such approaches does indeed exist and that 'they can be used to meet the varied and complex needs presented by children and young people who come into residential care' (*ibid.*, p. 197). The success of such interventions is often dependent on the quality of staff—resident relationships and as such would appear to provide an appropriate template for practice.

Holistic therapeutic approaches include the therapeutic community which is a specialised residential unit for young people which usually has education onsite and where intervention is organised on the basis of offering planned therapeutic help and support over the long term. Stevens and Furnivall (2008) highlight how the theoretical base of the therapeutic community is explicitly psychodynamic, where the existence of and effects of the unconscious mind are key concepts within the rationale of interventions for these establishments. Therapeutic communities follow many different approaches, with perhaps the one common element being that they are based on the need for staff to understand child development and the impact of early separation, deprivation and trauma.

Campling and Hague (1999) recount how various types of therapeutic communities evolved in the United Kingdom during the twentieth century. The work of such communities is under-researched and in the words of Ward *et al.* (2003, p. 13), 'in today's "evidence-based" terms its effectiveness is still technically unproven ...'. Little and Kelly's (1995) research into the Caldecott Community found that it provided as much stability as any other option. Figures indicated that children from 'fragmented families or exhibiting behavioural difficulties' were the most likely to do well, compared with children who were the victims of long-term abuse (Little and Kelly, 1995, p. 178).

Nevertheless, therapeutic approaches in residential care are not necessarily about an all-encompassing philosophy, such as that practised within therapeutic communities. Indeed, as Stevens and Furnivall (2008, p. 200) put it, 'the therapeutic use of daily life events in residential settings has been highlighted in the literature and perhaps constitutes a more naturalistic approach than therapeutic communities'. Opportunity-led work (Ward, 2000) or working in the *lifespace* are approaches which have been utilised at various points. 'Working in the *lifespace*' involves the conscious use of the everyday opportunities that present themselves in residential work, to engage meaningfully with young people about what is happening in their lives. A key aspect is the opportunity for the development of close working relationships between young people and staff, with practitioners building up knowledge and understanding of the young people's personal histories in order to make sense of their behaviours in the present. Such relationships can be extremely positive. The creation of a therapeutic *milieu* by staff is essential in order to implement effective lifespace interventions – the 'feel' of the unit. A range of factors will affect the milieu and might include the physical design, the organisational culture or the composition of resident and staff group (Stevens and Furnivall, 2008, p. 202).

Such approaches seem to point to a positive way forward for residential care, a way in which often troubled young people can be worked with in a way which is both empowering and productive of desirable outcomes. However, as highlighted by Stevens and Furnivall (2008), given the relative powerlessness of young people in residential care, it is important that residential staff and their parent organisations should be careful that they obtain permission from young people to work with them using such approaches, and that 'staff members and managers are clear and explicit about the reasons for the approaches being used' (*ibid.*, p. 207).

Gender in residential care

O'Neill (2008) summarises previous research which found gender differences in the experience of living in residential care and, whilst outcomes for both boys and girls remain poor overall, there is evidence that they are worse for girls. It is highlighted that policy and practice in recent years has resulted in the majority of residential homes accommodating boys and girls together, although it has been shown that any benefits of this 'normalising' arrangement are predominantly benefits for boys, with girls' needs subordinated or unrecognised, even where they are the majority in homes (Berridge and Brodie 1998; Farmer and Pollock 1998, cited in O'Neill, 2008). O'Neill concludes by stating that while boys and girls looked after in residential children's homes share some common concerns and experience of disadvantage, and experience the risks, problems and outcomes associated with placement in residential care:

> However, they (girls) also face problems and have needs which are unique to their gender and there has been little recognition that the needs of girls may be different from those of boys, or that alternative approaches and policies may be needed to respond to them. This has compounded the marginalisation of already socially excluded girls in

institutional care, who are expected to 'fit into' provision primarily designed for boys, resulting in even worse outcomes than their male peers (O'Neill, 2008, p. 102).

It is important to consider the individual needs of boys *and* girls in order for residential care to be a positive experience for both genders.

Minority ethnic children

Children from black and minority ethnic backgrounds and those of mixed parentage are disproportionately represented in the care system (Singh, 2005). Only a small number of studies have focused on their experiences in care, and an even smaller number on residential care (Kendrick, 2008). However, there has been clear evidence over the years that individual and institutional racism has been a central issue. Smith (2009) points to research suggesting that they are also faced with assumptions and practices that derive from specifically western bio-psycho-social perspectives (Singh, 2005) which impose a particular image of family, for instance locating it at a nuclear rather than an inter-generational level. Nevertheless, research by Barter *et al.* highlighted that positive practice and training can make significant inroads into the issue of racism in residential care:

> It was notable that racism was one area where staff were well prepared in these homes. Most homes had multi-cultural staff groups, and there were clear anti-racism policies ... with which both young people and staff were familiar. There were clearly-stated sanctions against racism of which young people were aware, and staff had often received in-service training on how to deal with racism'
> (Barter *et al.*, 2004, p. 215)

This is clearly an issue which requires ongoing attention and, 'residential workers and managers have a crucial role in providing positive culturally-specific experiences for the children and young people in their care, in supporting the development of their cultural and ethnic identity and in assisting young people in their transitions to adulthood' (Kendrick, 2008, p. 131).

Policy developments

Chapter 2 provides an overview and discussion of the historical development of the care system, including past and recent policy developments, both of which encompass residential care. The *Care Matters* White Paper (2007) endorsed residential care as having an important role to play as part of a range of placement options, particularly for older children. However, foster or kinship care is again clearly stated as being the ideal for the majority, thus retaining the existing hierarchy of placements. Nevertheless, that White Paper goes on to state that:

> It is therefore essential that the reforms focus on ensuring that the residential sector provides good quality care and that it is a valued and dynamic setting, able to support children in their development and enable them to move on where appropriate. (2007, p. 57)

The need to improve the training of residential care staff is emphasised, along with the potential value of the popular European model of residential child care, social pedagogy. A pilot programme, which ended in 2011, evaluated its effectiveness in the British residential care context (Berridge *et al.*, 2011) and which is described further in Chapter 7. Here, there is a clear acknowledgement that the current state of British residential care provision is far from ideal and requires much work in order to bring it up to an acceptable standard.

The current Coalition Government has stated that local authorities should see residential care as a positive placement option rather than as a last resort, and speaking on 18 July 2011, Children's Minister Tim Loughton said:

> For many children, residential children's homes offer stability and security they may have been missing in their early lives. Excellent residential care has the potential to turn children's lives around. We want to make sure all children's homes are up to the standard of the best and make sure that local authorities are considering them as a viable placement option if appropriate for certain children.

He went on to state the government's intention to work closely with sector on a programme of work to target underperforming children's homes. Nevertheless, given the pervasive problems that exist in the sector, it will remain to be seen whether much impact can be made on outcomes and attitudes, particularly in a climate where cuts are being made across public sector finances. Indeed, Utting (1997, p. 22) states that, 'the persistent deficiencies in children's homes are symptoms of a lack of commitment by political and service managers to unpopular, expensive but necessary provision' and goes on to point out that:

> Factors in the general background against which social services departments operate ... continue to work against residential care ... The financial pressures on social services through the general restraint on local authority spending expose the high unit costs of residential

care to continuous critical scrutiny. General arguments in favour of alternative services are heavily weighted by consideration of cost' (Utting, 1997, p. 23)

It will therefore remain to be seen whether current initiatives are any more successful than those which have gone before.

Conclusion

This chapter has provided an overview of the current residual residential care sector in the United Kingdom, looking at how the retrenchment of local authority provision has resulted in a burgeoning private sector, with many children being placed out of area, away from family and friends. The macro theoretical perspectives of Goffman (1961) and Foucault (1977) provided potential insights into the behaviour of young people and professionals in the institutional context. The impact of inquiries into abuse in residential care was seen, and the way that subsequent regulation of the sector has engendered defensive, 'back-covering' practice with children, while failing to address how perceptions of and attitudes towards young people in residential care can precipitate abuse in the first place. A discussion of life in residential care revealed how factors such as peer relationships and the group dynamics and culture of individual homes, staff-resident relationships, responses to challenging behaviour, and race and gender can have a profound impact on experiences and outcomes for the children and young people, in both positive and negative ways.

For a significant number of young people, a residential unit will be their placement of first choice; it is therefore imperative that it should be as positive an experience as possible.

5   Being adopted

Issues and controversies on the road to permanence

> My brother is about 7 and he is up for adoption. He doesn't even know
> that I have a daughter and that he is an uncle. We can send letters, but
> letters aren't enough.
>
> > (Jennifer, in care late 1990s and 2000s)

The issue of adoption is a crucial element of child welfare practice and
policy. Adoption can act as a placement that avoids the care system and also
as a route out of care that can offer stability and permanence for children
and young people:

> ... permanence through adoption gives a child a replacement family.
> The intention is to replicate in law 'normal' (birth) family life and
> relationships (Luckock and Hart, 2005, p. 127).

Unfortunately adoption can also sometimes provide a route back into care
following the breakdown of adoption placements. This chapter will offer
an analysis of adoption and how it links to other elements of the child
welfare system; with a particular focus on young people and the impact of
adoption on them and their life course. Here we consider the many
challenges and controversies implicit in the process of adoption, drawing
on recent policy debates, with particular reference to issues around ethnicity
and adoption.

Controversies

There can be little doubt that adoption is a controversial and challenging
form of child welfare practice. As Simmonds states: 'adoption as a policy

issue attracts the most intense public interest' (2012, p. 174). Each stage of the adoption process raises some sort of controversy, for example:

- which children and young people should be placed for adoption?
- when should they be placed for adoption?
- who is suitable to be an adopter?
- how should children be matched with those identified as potential adopters?
- what support, if any, should be offered to adoptive placements?
- what are the outcomes of adoption?

Each of these questions is controversial, and potentially supportable on either side by research findings and statistics. Underpinning these questions are many of the central issues that are the subject of this book – issues that can be summarised as being ultimately about how we conceptualise the relationship between the State and the family. These questions will be explored here using the influential framework provided by Martin Narey (Narey, 2011) in a report which was instrumental in his appointment as an adoption advisor, or 'adoption tsar', for the UK government. In his report Narey presents adoption as a potential solution to many of the challenges facing the care system and in doing so explores a number of useful themes for exploring the questions listed above.

Adoption is relevant to young people who are the subject of this book in a number of ways – some may have been adopted as babies, some adopted as children and others will be considered for adoption during their teenage years. When young people themselves have been adopted they will reflect on the experience of adoption in their own unique way relating to their own personal history and narrative. Whatever these narratives are, an 'adopted identity' will have an impact on how young people understand and construct their own life course and identity (Harris, 2006).

It should also be recalled that the impact of adoption spreads wider than those who have actually been adopted – a high proportion of the readership of this book will have at least one friend, relative or a partner who has been adopted or will know of an adoptive family. The impact of adoption on modern western societies is therefore extensive, as reflected in the frequent representation of adoption in cultural forms such as in fiction, 'soap operas' and films. Adoption has a popular presence in many cultural forms which is often related to dramatic disclosures about who someone's biological parents are (see Mike Leigh's film 'Secrets and Lies', for example). Adoption also has a resonance in the popular news media that often carry stories about issues such as 'obese' people who have been rejected as potential adopters, or where ethnic factors have been alleged to be a barrier to adoption. In recent years attention has also been paid to international adoption, particularly where this has a 'celebrity' element (Madonna; Brad Pitt and Angelina Jolie).

Adoption: challenge and contention

Throughout 2011 *The Times* ran a high-profile campaign about adoption: the topic appeared on the front page of many editions accompanied by a series of features on many aspects of adoption. The basic tenets of the campaign were as follows:

- more children and young people should be adopted
- the process should be speedier and more efficient
- the approval of potential adopters should be more open and flexible
- the emphasis on 'same race' matching should be decreased.

The Times commissioned a report from Martin Narey, who was later appointed as the government's special advisor on adoption. The UK government accepted the basic arguments of *The Times*' campaign as a basis for policy during 2012 (Department for Education, 2012). The main points of that clearly influential report (Narey, M. (2011) *Narey Report on Adoption*, Supplement to *The Times*, 5 July), underpins the structure of this chapter. The fact that *The Times* chose to run this campaign at all illustrates that many of the issues and controversies that are inherent to adoption policy and practice have a popular resonance.

The Narey approach has a clear lineage which we can see in a report published by the free market thinktank, the Institute of Economic Affairs, written by Patricia Morgan ('Adoption and the Care of Children', 1998). The tone of the Narey report can be seen to be taking its cue from passages like this (opening passage) from Morgan's report:

> Adoption has fallen out of favour. It is presented negatively ... Numbers have fallen dramatically, and baby adoptions have become rare events. The unmarried mother is now asked to choose between abortion and lone parenthood, with adoption scarcely mentioned as an option ... (local authorities) make few adoption placements, and place all sorts of obstacles in the way of couples wanting to adopt
>
> (1998, p. 1)

This line of argument is explored further in this chapter, which concludes with a longer, illustrative discussion of the topic of 'same race' and 'transracial' adoption – arguably the single most controversial aspect of adoption.

A brief history of adoption

Adoption has a long history, with examples to be found in the Bible and in Roman history. Boswell in his study of abandoned children and 'the kindness of strangers' demonstrates that 'adoption was, in fact, extremely common in the early [Roman] empire' (1988, p. 115). Adoption usually occurred without the State playing a role. In many Western countries this began to change during the 1920s when concern began to grow about the supervision of children and about the possibility of children being bought and sold for money or goods. Following the First World War (1914–18) there were also concerns about the care and protection of 'war orphans'. In Britain these concerns led to the Adoption Act 1926 which enhanced the role of the State in the regulation of adoption. From this period until the 1960s a primary concern was that children stigmatised by being born to unmarried mothers were given a chance of being brought up by a married couple. Following the Act, throughout the 1930s, the number of adoptions was around 5,000 per annum and consisted largely of baby adoptions, with the child being removed from the birth mother immediately following birth.

In Britain concerns about 'baby farming' (the breastfeeding of groups of babies by one woman; Fildes, 1988) and a need to regulate adoption agencies led to appointment of the Horsbrugh Committee on Adoption in 1936. This in turn led to the 1939 Adoption of Children (Regulation) Act which increased the regulation of adoption agencies, particularly in relation to restrictions on advertising children for reward. The Act also, importantly, established that adoption should be in the 'best interests of the child.' The Second World War and political factors delayed the actual implementation of the Act until 1943.

As we have seen, adoption during this period was seen as a route out of 'shame and stigma' for single mothers – although it should be noted that in fact a significant proportion of children born within marriages were also adopted. Certainly adoption was seen as something for babies – and not for the older young people who are the primary focus of this book.

Through the late 1960s and into the 1970s we see a decline in the number of adoptions (see Parker, 1999, p. 1). In the United Kingdom there were more than 20,000 adoptions per annum through the 1960s, which then fell steadily and was less than 10,000 per annum in 1983. The number of adoptions seems to have plateaued at just above 3,000 a year during the decade of the 2000s. The causes of this decline are widely documented and include the increased availability of the contraceptive pill and of abortion, wider acceptance of single parenthood, women having increased economic ability to act as single parents and to make independent lifestyle decisions: 'as a result of these converging trends, the character of unmarried motherhood underwent a radical transformation' (Parker, 1999, p. 2) which in turn led to a change in the profile of adoption. Thus during the 1960s the nature of adoption began to shift, and with the reduced availability of newborn babies, potential adopters began to look at two groups previously considered largely 'unadoptable' – black children and older children with care experience.

In summary then, from the first decades of the twentieth century we have seen a shift in adoption policy and practice – from a service provided largely to place newborn babies with married couples to, later in the century, a much more complex and wide-ranging service, largely focused on children in the care system. There was also a shift in attitudes towards the care of vulnerable children during this period with a concern about 'drift in care' which was sharpened by the publication of a key publication 'Children Who Wait' (Rowe and Lambert, 1973). It became accepted that long periods in the care system, particularly in residential care, were unhelpful; young people need careful care planning leading to a permanent solution for them. The argument for a stronger permanency planning for children in care became dominant and influenced the UK Children Act 1975, and the Adoption Act 1976.

Professional attitudes to adoption

Why then is adoption currently regarded as controversial? The Narey report wants to promote more positive and pro-active attitudes to adoption and as a result develops the strong permanency position highlighted by Rowe and Lambert (*ibid.*). Narey is a proponent of an active, if not aggressive, pro-adoption stance. He argues that three professional attitudes act as a barrier to increasing the number, and speed, of adoptions:

* (mis)interpretations of attachment theory
* perspectives on parental rights, and
* the perceived negative consequences of coming into care.

Let us examine each of these attitudes in turn.

First, attachment theory. Discussions of attachment theory are clearly relevant to adoption – in fact the entire adoption process rests on the assumption that it is possible to form positive new attachments with substitute carers. John Bowlby, utilising a psycho-analytical perspective, famously argued that the attachment between the newborn infant and it's mother is crucial to the growing child's mental health. He pointed out that the negative consequences of maternal deprivation which occurs:

* during the period of separation
* during the period immediately after restoration to maternal care, and
* in at least a small proportion of cases permanently (1953, p. 53)

Writing in a post-Second World War 'pro-family' climate, Bowlby's work became influential and was popularised through BBC broadcasts such as those by D. W. Winnicot. This perspective therefore provided a focus on the mother–child bond, suggesting that placement with an alternative carer would be undesirable (in destroying this bond), and also unsuccessful (the bond could not be reproduced or replaced). The ideological deployment of attachment theory also had arguably politically regressive consequences: placing an emphasis on the mother remaining at home with the child, contributing to the closure of wartime nurseries and distancing the father from child care (Frost and Stein, 1989). What we might call this 'reductionist' attachment theory was revised in the work of Sir Michael Rutter. He demonstrated that the main attachment could indeed be with a father, and that an alternative attachment with a substitute carer could be achieved. Rutter argued that attachment began at seven months of age, and was not simply biological in nature, but dependent on the warmth of the attachment. He also argued that stability mattered, an argument later developed by Rowe and Lambert, and pointed to the dangers of a variety of carers in the early years leading to disorganised attachments and to problems later in life.

The care experience of young people therefore raises a number of issues about attachment and stability and which underpin some of the controversial debates about adoption. Certainly Narey argues that misunderstandings of attachment theory act as a barrier to the appropriate use of adoption.

The second barrier to adoption, according to Narey, is an over-emphasis on the 'rights of parents'. Parental responsibilities (as opposed to rights) are often enshrined in legislation and represent a major battlefield between the State and the family (see Frost, 2011) – for example in relation to issues such as physical chastisement and what is 'good enough parenting'. The United Nations Charter of Human Rights is often quoted in this context. The Charter promotes 'the right to respect for [his] private and family life, [his] home and [his] correspondence'. This formulation seems to privilege the 'right to family life' over other rights. There are also possible tensions between an emphasis on family life with the 'paramountcy' of the rights of the child, where specific aspects of family life can be seen as harmful to children. The concept of paramountcy again draws on the UN Convention on the Rights of the Child and is enshrined, for example in the UK Children Act 1989, which clearly stipulates the 'paramountcy of the child's welfare'.

The perspective taken by Martin Narey and others is over-simplistic in arguing that 'paramountcy' of children should outweigh 'respect for family life', but more seriously it is an error to assume that the paramountcy of the child's welfare equates with adoption. This cannot be argued as an abstract case as Narey attempts – but is actually dependent on the careful exploration of the concrete individual situation, which is indeed the everyday task of family court practice across the planet. Indeed there is a danger in adults defining abstractly 'the best interests of the child', in any situation.

The third barrier identified by Narey is that professionals strive to keep children with their birth family because being in care is seen as a negative experience and is associated with poor outcomes for children and young people. Narey wishes to challenge this view and quotes Stein's argument that: 'the simplistic view of care failing ... young people should be confined to the dustbin' (Stein, 2006).

Narey quotes research from Farmer and Lutman and Wade *et al.* (both in Davies and Ward, 2012) to help establish his position that professionals are reluctant to utilise the care system and that being in care can be associated with positive outcomes. Farmer and Lutman attempt to illustrate professionals' reluctance to utilise the care system by demonstrating that:

> Three-fifths of referrals about harm did not lead to sufficient action. Decisive action often awaited a trigger incident of physical/sexual abuse or severe domestic violence. Over time abuse and neglect were sometimes minimised Farmer and Lutman, in Davies and Ward, 2012, p. 175.

They argue that the care system can be successful as:

> After five years, 43 per cent of the children were stably at home, 29 per cent had achieved permanence away from home, whilst 28 per cent had unstable experiences in care or at home. Those living stably away from home were more likely to have good overall wellbeing. (Farmer and Lutman, in Davies and Ward, 2012, p. 175).

Wade *et al.* (in Davies and Ward, 2012) also demonstrate that the outcomes for children in care – in terms of stability and wellbeing are better than those who returned home to their birth families:

> Outcomes for maltreated children who remained looked after were better than for those who went home, with respect to stability and wellbeing. Even those whose home placements had endured had lower wellbeing than those who had not gone home. (p. 192)

Thus Narey argues that these three barriers – attitudes to attachment theory, parents' rights, and attitudes to the care experience – all undermine the role of adoption in child welfare. He goes on to argue that there is therefore a widespread antipathy to adoption in the United Kingdom, a position also taken by traditional conservative commentators such as Patricia Morgan. Narey argues that:

> ...the relative marginalisation of adoption in the UK reflects a growing antipathy on the part of an increasing number of practitioners and academics. Misunderstandings about the effect of state intervention, human rights legislation and attachment theory have contributed to that ... (2011, p. 7).

As a result of this professional antipathy he goes on to argue that:

> Certainly adoption is not a high-profile option for women unable to raise their own children where the choice is often presented as being between abortion and raising their own child (Narey, 2011, p. 7).

One of the issues raised by Narey, and later pursued by British Prime Minister David Cameron, is that of delay in the adoption process. This had also been flagged by the previous Prime Minister, Tony Blair (2000). Delay remains a major issue that has not been tackled by the implementation of the 1989 Children Act and subsequent reforms such as the Public Law Outline. In the English 'Review of Family Justice' (2011) it is argued that: 'Cases now take a length of time that is little short of scandalous'.

Even where babies are placed for adoption at birth it is unlikely that proceedings will be completed before their first birthday due to delays in the court system. Delay is however a complex issue – it may involve a decision to remove the child, a decision whether adoption is suitable, or matching a child with potential adopters. All of these can take time as can the intricacies of legal and court processes.

Post-adoption support

In his report Martin Narey goes on to examine the issue of adoption breakdown: an issue often underplayed by pro-adoption campaigners. There is some dispute about the rate of adoption breakdown. In the studies summarised and outlined by Parker (1999), breakdown rates vary from two per cent to 24 per cent. National official data is not collected, fuelling uncertainty in this area. However, this issue is explored by Rushton and Dance (2006) who researched adoption of children aged 5–11. The children were tracked until their 14th birthday by which time 23 per cent of adoptive placements had broken down. Narey also reports Rutter's study of 165 adoptions of Romanian children where two broke down after being followed until their 14th birthday. Again we can see that this is a controversial aspect of adoption.

Adoption breakdown raises the issue of post-adoption support which has gained a higher profile in recent decades. The importance of support following adoption is highlighted by Parker:

> Many children placed for adoption will have experienced numerous prior disruptions which may have damaged their self-esteem or confidence and made them wary of placing too much reliance upon new attachments. For such children the multiple nature of the re-adjustments which they are called upon are daunting. They will need support (1999, p. 76).

The 2002 Adoption and Children Act promotes post-adoption support, as does the 2012 'An Action Plan for Adoption: Tackling Delay' (Department for Education, 2012). However, Luckock and Hart detect an ambiguity and ambivalence in state policy towards adoption support. This ambivalence, they argue, rests in the tension between the adoptive family replicating the birth family whilst also representing a form 'reparative parenting' (2005, p. 127). They argue, persuasively, that this ambivalence can be detected in both academic analysis and policy approaches to adoption support. They conclude by arguing that: 'Adoption is a different way of "doing" family life and the nature of that difference must be understood if services are to be effective' (Luckock and Hart, 2005, p. 133).

If this position is accepted it follows that there is a clear role for adoption support services and for exploring how effective these are. Rushton conducted a randomised controlled trial (RCT) of adoption support (Rushton & Monck, Thirty-seven families participated in this study and were allocated to three groups:

1   one group received behavioural parenting advice
2   another received a parenting advice programme aimed at adoptive parents, and
3   there was a third 'service as usual' control group (the usual adoption service). This group was offered an additional service on completion of the research so that they were not disadvantaged.

The method was to gather information using standardised questionnaires (e.g. a Strengths and Difficulties Questionnaire) and qualitative interviews before the intervention, immediately after the intervention and six months later. The findings were mixed: for example: 'parenting changes were more apparent in the combined intervention groups than the control group'

(2009, p. 2) but that 'no significant differences between groups were found when the baseline data were compared with the post-intervention data or when baseline data were compared with six-month post-intervention data' (2009, p. 3). The research team also undertook a cost effectiveness study. This concluded that: 'combining overall costs [of social care provision] with differences in outcomes showed a cost of £731 per unit improvement in "satisfaction with parenting" in the short term and £337 in the longer term' (2009, p. 3). Overall, the study, whilst recognising the limitations of a relatively small-scale study, concluded that data related to the provision of additional services were positive:

> ... the findings suggest that a home-based parenting programme for adopters caring for children with substantial emotional and behavioural problems in the first 18 months of placement resulted in positive changes in parenting satisfaction and less negative parenting approaches (2009, p. 4).

Adoption and ethnicity – child welfare and political controversy

Perhaps predominant in the list of controversies in terms of profile and contestability is the issue of trans-racial adoption (TRA), again this issue was flaggedin the Narey Report (2011), where again Narey's stance is powerfully stated:

> The now long-established determination to find the right ethnic match for a child is ... based on a dubious emphasis on culture and heritage - particularly when talking about a baby – and is certainly and demonstrably damaging to black and mixed-race children, where delay is persistent and unacceptable (2011, p. 12).

The issue of TRA raises many fundamental questions: When should a child be placed for adoption and with whom? What is a good enough family? How can children and young people in care be given positive images of who they are? It also raises many of the wider fundamental issues of our age such as ethnicity, identity, social class and family.

We will approach this controversial issue as follows:

- first we will examine the social history of TRA
- second we look at relevant research and theory
- third we explore recently-published UK government guidance as an example of political response to the controversy.

The social history of TRA

The history of TRA can perhaps be usefully seen as falling into four historical periods.

The 'Colour Blind' period

The 1950s and 1960s were characterised by liberal approaches to adoption. Those who arrived from the West Indies in boats like he 'Windrush' sometimes experienced the ups and downs of life in a new culture, and the care system in United Kingdom found itself caring for more black children and young people. White adopters were asked to come forward – some readers will know people who adopted, or who were adopted, during the period – black children raised in white families. Many of these children have written and spoken about their experiences – in poems, novels and memoirs (Harris, 2006), as we will see later. The predominant ideology of the period we can describe as 'colour blind'. By this we mean that people felt that white carers could effectively raise black children – that love and care were more important than ethnicity. This was a liberal and well-meaning approach, aimed at giving the best possible life for black children who otherwise would have been in long-term residential care.

The multi-cultural period

This 'colour blind' approach was critiqued – by black professionals, black political groups and by young people themselves who were trans-racially adopted. As the 1960s progressed and we entered the 1970s multi-cultural approaches became stronger. Here the perception changed from the 'colour doesn't matter' narrative outlined above to one that recognised the importance of culture and heritage but believed that such issues could be successfully addressed by new white families. Here it was considered that children of all cultures could be successfully raised by white carers as long as those carers addressed their cultural needs and interests. Such children could be brought up to be proud of who they were, were in touch with their roots and heritage and could be resilient when they experienced racism. We had moved on from a 'colour blind' approach to a 'melting pot' approach – with black and white people living together and caring for each other.

Same race adoption period

During the late-1960s and the1970s the voice of anti-racism and the Black Liberation movement in the United States became louder and more insistent.

The 'colour blind' approach was by now discredited and multi-culturalism was seen as not delivering effective care for black young people. Multi-cultural approaches were seen as transferring black children to white families and allowing white people to set the cultural agenda. The anti-racist movement considered that only black carers should care for black children and that this would produce the best outcomes for young people: in terms of their resilience, sense of identity, pride, positive self-image and ability to tackle racism. Political and professional groups became radically opposed to TRA – now seen as a social transfer market in black children to white families, and seriously undermined both individual welfare and black self-confidence as a collective form.

Post-modern approaches

In the 1990s a radical approach to TRA emerged. It used theories of post-modernity and identity to challenge the new political and professional orthodoxy that was against TRA. Such theories are complex and often difficult to grasp. They argue that none of us can be reduced to essential identities – we all have multiple identities (e.g., we might at the same time be a mother, a professional social worker and a long-distance runner) and people cannot be reduced to one identity and nor should one identity be privileged over another. For example, does a black working-class woman have more in common with a black man or a white working-class woman? Identities are also fluid and shift over time – 'being black' has multiple meanings and will have different implications say in a school classroom or in a night club, for example. These complexities become more pronounced when we consider mixed heritage children – should they be identified as black, as mixed heritage or should they be empowered to choose their own identity? Post-modern approaches would suggest that such changes are fluid and flexible: they cannot be reduced to essential identities. It follows that the simple formulation that 'black adopters' should care for 'black children' is unsustainable.

These four historical periods and perspectives should not be taken as rigid or historically fixed – but they help us to open up and understand debates and perspectives on the issue of TRA. Let us explore these debates in more depth.

Early British research into TRA children argued that:

> ...these black children have been white in all but skin colour ... have no contact with the black community and their 'coping' mechanisms are based on denying their racial background (Gill and Jackson, 1983, p. 137).

Here it is argued that TRA children lose their sense of self and pride in their colour, and they start to internalise negative self images:

> Many trans-racially adopted children are aware that the darker their skin colour the more undesirable they are to white society; and many feel that it is better to be white than black... (Small,1986, p. 82).

This is based on a sense that: 'If a healthy personality is to be formed, the psychic image of the child must merge with the reality of what the child actually is' (Small, 1986, p. 88).

The author of the last two quotes was John Small, a black senior manager in a London Borough, who was dominant in the arguments around TRA. He worked closely with a psychiatrist, Maxime, who provided therapeutic back up for Small's more political stance:

> Most black children being cared for by white caretakers, harbour negative attitudes either towards black people in general or to what they fantasize black people to be (1986, p. 105).

These are powerful and strong critiques of TRA – being both uncompromising and politically informed. One may argue that the issue of dual heritage makes these issues more complex, but again Small is typically uncompromising on this:

> The concept of mixed race, which has become part of conventional social work language is misleading because it causes confusion in the minds of trans-racial adopters. It can lead them to believe that such children are racially distinct from other blacks (Small, 1986, p. 91).

These are powerful arguments against TRA, often backed up by the first person testimony of TRA young people (see Harris, 2006).

In order to shed light on the issue of dual heritage young people the English Department of Health commissioned an in-depth study undertaken by Tizard and Phoenix during the early 1990s. They challenge John Small about his use of the concept 'black' as follows:

> Small seems to assume that there is a unitary black culture shared by black people irrespective of their gender, age, social class or country of origin (Tizard and Phoenix, 1993, p. 175).

Tizard and Phoenix go on to argue that 'colour' should not be privileged in terms of identity:

.... our findings suggest that the colour of the parents is likely to have less impact on their child's development than their attitudes towards colour and racism, and their social class' (Tizard and Phoenix, 1993, p. 176).

This is a more fluid, less essentialist, approach to TRA and is utilised by Kirton who argues that:

... in recent years, drawing on wider debate on 'postmodernism' and the critique of 'essentialism', there have been attempts to problematize the notions of identity and culture which lie at the heart of the orthodoxy (Kirton, 2000, p. 124).

An important commentator on this issue from a sociological point of view is the eminent black sociologist Paul Gilroy, who expresses his surprise at the emphasis placed on TRA issues:

... the feeling (these issues) arouse seem somehow out of proportion when seen in relation to the more profound and more intractable problems of poverty, crime, drug misuse and social, economic and political marginalisation that arise in a racially structured society (Gilroy,1994, p. ix).

We can see how controversial these issues are. But how do these debates translate into contemporary policy and practice approaches? This issue will be explored in the remainder of this chapter.

Government guidance on ethnicity and adoption

Soon after coming to power in 2010 the Coalition Government issued Guidance on adoption practice, which it clearly saw as a priority issue in which Prime Minister David Cameron played a primary role. It should be noted that relatively little of this Guidance addresses issues around ethnicity, although this was what attracted much of the media attention. The Minister for Children, Tim Loughton, made his position clear in the Introduction, which is worth quoting at some length:

I want to move away from the situation where children are kept in care for a long time simply to find a family of the same ethnicity when a suitable family of a different ethnic background is available who can meet their other needs. To say the obvious, parents from one particular background can be loving, sensitive and successful adoptive parents for children from very different backgrounds and that must be our primary consideration. Local authorities must consider all of the child's needs and not place the issue of ethnicity above everything else, though this must be taken into account. I know that children tend to do well when placed with a family who shares their ethnic or cultural background, but I know also that delay can have a very detrimental effect. It reduces the child's chances of finding a family and has negative consequences on their future development. If there can be an ethnic match that's an advantage, possibly a very significant one. But, it should never be a 'dealbreaker' (Tim Loughton, Introduction, Department for Education, 2011).

The language here is careful and thoughtful – perhaps until the use of the final colloquialism. By the headlining of the issue in the Introduction it is clear that the government is attempting to shift the emphasis in ethnically-matched placements. This position was clarified in 'An Action Plan for Adoption' as follows (Department for Education, 2012):

The delay faced by Black children ... needs particular attention. They take about a year longer to be adopted after entering care than White and Asian children. Capitals agreed One reason for this is that in some parts of the system, the belief persists that ensuring a perfect or near perfect match based on the child's ethnicity is necessarily in the child's best interests, and automatically outweighs other considerations, such as the need to find long-term stability for the child quickly (Department for Education, 2012, p. 21).

The Action Plan goes on to state that:

It is not in the best interests of children for social workers to introduce any delay at all into the adoption process in the search for a perfect or even partial ethnic match when parents who are otherwise suitable are available and able to provide a loving and caring home for the child (Department for Education, 2012, p. 22).

Let us examine how the actual Guidance approaches this issue. It is stated that:

Agencies must not turn away potential adopters whose ethnicity and culture is not shared with those of the children waiting to be placed with adoptive parents.

While children do tend to do better if adopted by a family who shares their ethnic origin or cultural group, these are just one of many considerations and must not be the primary consideration. A prospective adopter is able to parent a child with whom they do not share the same ethnicity, provided they can meet the child's other identified needs. The agency must provide them with flexible and creative support. This applies equally whether a child is placed with a black or minority ethnic family, a white family, or a family which includes members of different ethnic origins. *It is unacceptable for a child to be denied adoptive parents solely on the grounds that the child and prospective adopter do not share the same racial or cultural background*

(emphasis in the original, 3.16, Department for Education, 2011).

The Guidance becomes more strident here: this closes off the emphasis on same race adoption. The argument goes on to be influenced by the non-essentialist thinking that we have examined earlier:

The structure of white, black and minority ethnic groups is often complex and their heritage diverse, where the race, religion, language and culture of each community has varying degrees of importance in the daily lives of individuals. It is important that social workers avoid 'labelling' a child and ignoring some elements in their background, or placing the child's ethnicity above all else when looking for an adoptive family for the child (emphasis in the original, 3.16, Department for Education, 2011).

The Guidance goes on to explore in some detail what good practice with a trans-racially adopted child may look like. This section is reminiscent of our earlier discussion of multi-cultural approaches:

All families should help children placed with them to understand and appreciate their background and culture. Where the child and prospective adopter do not share the same background, the prospective adopter will need flexible and creative support from their agency. This should be in the form of education and training, not just simplistic advice, provided in a vacuum, on learning their children's cultural traditions or about the food/cooking from their birth heritage. The support plan should consider how the child's understanding of their background and origin might be enhanced. This can include providing opportunities for children to meet others from similar backgrounds, and to practise their religion – both in a formal place of worship and in the home. Maintaining continuity of the heritage of their birth family is important to most children; it is a means of retaining knowledge of their identity and feeling that although they have left their birth family they have not abandoned important cultural, religious or linguistic values of their community. This will be of particular significance as they reach adulthood (4.8, Department for Education, 2011).

This Guidance is significant and may represent another historical shift in adoption practice in relation to ethnicity. However, the controversies around race and adoption will, no doubt, continue.

Good practice in work with looked-after minority ethnic children and young people

So where does this debate leave us in terms of actual professional practice with children and young people? Again we can find contrasting positions in the literature and campaigning material. Perlita Harris states that 'too many trans-racially adopted adults report feeling alienated, displaced and disconnected from their community of origin ... the narratives of trans-racially adopted adults demonstrate unequivocally that love alone is simply not enough' (www.minorityperspective.co.uk 2 November 2010)

By contrast Silverman, drawing on a range of empirical studies, argues that trans-racial adoption:

> ...appears to produce children whose self-esteem is at least as high as that of non-adopted children and whose adjustment is highly satisfactory (1993, p. 117).

The US-based Evan B. Donaldson Institute takes a more nuanced position:

> Trans-racial adoption in itself does not produce psychological or social maladjustment problems in children.
>
> Trans-racially adopted children and their families face a range of challenges, and the manner in which parents handle them facilitates or hinders children's development.
>
> Children in foster care come to adoption with many risk factors that pose challenges for healthy development. For these children, research points to the importance of adoptive placements with families who can address their individual issues and maximize their opportunity to develop to their fullest potential (Evan. B. Donaldson Institute, 2008, p. 5).

Lee develops this more nuanced and personalised position and argues that:

> Practitioners must begin with an understanding of the history and controversies that surround TRA.

They need to dispel any myths that surround TRA.

They need to understand the specific way that the TRA paradox plays out in any given situation (Lee, 2003, p. 23).

Thus instead of regarding children and young people as objects of policy, Lee suggests that: 'Perhaps most important, practitioners should view trans-racial adoptees and families as active agents of change in their personal and social lives' (2003, p. 23).

This has implications for practice and for practice skills we need to develop:

'Culturally competent practitioners can serve as cultural brokers who help trans-racial adoptees and adoptive parents identify and resolve these differences' (Lee, 2003, p. 23).

This has profound implications for professional training and practice development.

Conclusion

We have seen how adoption is a controversial and challenging topic in child welfare. It is an issue that is central for many young people: those who have been adopted, those who may be adopted in the future and the many who have adopted friends and family members. We have seen that adoption has a wide resonance socially – both in the empirical sense that the lives of many people are touched in some way by adoption, but also in the theoretical sense that the 'discourse' around adoption is socially significant in terms of debates about the family, parenting, ethnicity and social class.

Adoption will no doubt continue to be politically controversial for some time to come.

6 Leaving care and the transition to adulthood

The acid test of the care system?

> When I moved to semi-independence my permanent social worker has been brilliant, when I phone she calls me straight back, and comes and sees me, she is like a friend to me. She talks to me like I'm an adult.
> (Chelsea, in care 1990 and 2000s)

A key issue for young people with experience of the care system, and for those working with them, is the experience of 'leaving care', an experience known as 'ageing out of care' or 'emancipation from care' in the United States. Whatever its label, it is concerned with the nature of the transition to adulthood, which is a shared experience for all young people, regardless of whether or not they have been in care. For all young people in post-industrial societies the process of transition to adulthood is becoming more complex, 'The transition to adulthood is increasingly being postponed and becoming less standardised' (Berrington, Stone and Falkingham, 2009, p. 27).

Whereas previous generations have experienced a close connection between leaving home, marriage and gaining employment this is for contemporary young people an increasingly disconnected series of events. This chapter aims to explore the nature of the transition to adulthood for young people who are care experienced, and the factors that have an impact on its success or otherwise.

The transition of young people to adulthood is a complex and challenging process for young people leaving care:

> ... young people making the journey from care to adulthood often have more accelerated and compressed transitions to adulthood than their peers, and are more likely to be disadvantaged in respect to the main pathways to adulthood (Stein and Ward, 2011, p. 2409).

Young people leaving care as a group are now subject to a significant amount of attention and research. This reflects a number of factors –

including the campaigning work of young people and their organisations, the pioneering work of a group of academics and the subsequent attention of policymakers (Stein, 2011).

Leaving care consists of three closely related processes. First of all the experience of young people whilst they are actually in care is fundamental to their future life course. Second, there is the actual experience of leaving care and how well this is planned and executed in practice. The third element of the leaving care process concerns after care and support, a stage at which the outcomes of the care system are often explored. In many ways a young person's experience of leaving care is the 'acid test' of the success or otherwise of being in care.

Being in care: the impact on life after care

It is argued here that an effective care experience for young people in the care system is underpinned by stability of placement, in a quality care setting, held together by effective and participative care planning. The nature of this experience will have a major impact on the prospects of young people once they have left care. It has been demonstrated by successful research (Stein, 2004) that there is a strong association between the stability of care placements and a successful transition to adulthood. This is neatly summarised here:

> For some young people in care, placement instability is known to have a damaging effect on a wide variety of outcomes, including education, and employment – not least because each new placement often means a new school and new friends. Difficult home circumstances can mean that, by the end of compulsory schooling, many young care leavers have such broken and incomplete attendance records that sitting exams is unthinkable. As a result, despite a recent focus on educational attainment and placement stability for children in care, they continue to attain qualifications below the level that is regarded as the basic threshold for employability. In England in 2008, for example only 13 per cent of children in care achieved five A* -C grade GCSEs, while in Scotland 16.7 per cent of young people looked after away from home had no qualifications at SCQF level 3+.16 These figures represent an improvement on previous years, but there is clearly still a long way to go (Action for Children, 2011, pp. 14–15)

The pervasive impact of placement instability can be seen here. Underpinning the stability of care placements are two key factors: successful care planning and the quality of placements.

There are four major aims for care planning in ensuring that:

- young people have a clear and shared plan for their future and are not subject to 'drift' (see Chapter 5)
- young people are fully involved and consulted about the key decisions concerning their lives
- the care system operates in an effective manner for the young person to ensure that young people achieve the best possible outcomes on leaving care
- change and transitions are successfully managed with the young person – in particular the transition to adulthood.

If these factors are in place it follows that placement instability should be reduced. In the English situation care planning is closely regulated through a set of central government regulations known as the 'Care Planning, Placement and Case Review Regulations' (Department for Education, 2010). The care planning process is seen as enabling professionals to deliver 'corporate parenting': the process by which professionals work together in the perceived best interests of the young person. This process is carried out under the overview of an Independent Reviewing Officer (IRO) who chairs the planning meetings, should meet with the young person beforehand and should have a key role in the life of a young person in care.

It is important that the care planning process varies in nature and content for each young person and in this sense should be 'personalised' to fit with them and their unique set of circumstances. It is also important to reflect on the place of foster care and residential care in care planning. The role of residential childcare has declined in recent decades, and social and professional attitudes have shifted against 'institutional' provision, in some countries it has become a 'residual' resource within the care system (see further Chapter 4). It is argued here that there are many problems with this approach, including the fact that young people themselves often speak of the positive aspects of residential care and the valuable role that it plays. Young people often emphasise their preference for residential care, for example, when they have experienced foster care breakdowns, when they wish to be placed in sibling groups or where they have close links with parents and as a result may not wish to establish a bond with substitute foster carers. This attitude is well-illustrated by the statement of Dawn Howley, who spent some of her childhood in care:

> Residential care is the only option for some children because foster care, which essentially mirrors a family unit, is often too frightening and painful for a child who has left a dysfunctional family. Residential

care is so important, and should be an equal option for children alongside fostering, because it has more boundaries and rules and regulations, which many young people might find annoying but do respond to, and the staff are carers rather than parents ... . (Howley, *The Guardian*, 2011)

Foster care offers a more personalised form of care and the nature of planning will differ from that in residential care. The children may well be younger than in residential care, although this is not necessarily the case. Clearly foster carers need to be closely involved in the planning process. In terms of preparation for leaving care it is important that there are a range of placement options available so that care planning can be effective in selecting the most suitable placement.

The important point to note is that for professional care planning to take place a range of resources needs to be available to support effective decision-making. If care is to be effective for young people there needs to be a real choice – with a range of placements available. The more stable and caring the young person's care experience is the more successful they are likely to be on leaving care.

Working with the young person

A fully effective care planning process places the young person at its centre – both in terms of ensuring that the best interests of the young person are actively pursued and in ensuring that young people participate as fully as possible in the process. A study by Thomas demonstrated why young people wanted to be involved in relevant decision making, with one young person in the study clearly stating 'it is our life – we have our own feelings, concerns and views, and the outcomes will affect us' (Thomas, 2000, p. 151).

Care planning is perhaps the most important tool for ensuring that the care system meets the needs of the young person and therefore contributes to their chances of success in leaving care (see Williams, 2005). The English National Institute for Clinical and Health Excellence (NICE) summarises the importance of care planning in these words:

Evidence indicates that effective care planning, led by social workers, promotes permanence and reduces the need for emergency placements and placement changes. Good care planning supports the quality of the relationship between the child or young person and carer by minimising disruption, increasing attachment and providing greater placement stability, which also helps promote a stable education (NICE, 2010, p. 19)

We suggest that the following steps are necessary to ensure that the needs of young people are met.

First, the planning process needs to be seen as a priority and it is important to make sure that the necessary time and resources are utilised in care planning. High-quality care planning needs careful preparation, with adequate time being dedicated and careful thought given to the requirements of the process.

Second, it is important that all relevant people are present at the review wherever possible. This also requires careful planning in relation to the timing of meetings, ensuring that the correct people are invited and that the venue is agreed by the young person and is both suitable and convenient.

Third, it is important that all the required information is available at the meeting. The care planning meeting will only be truly effective if relevant paperwork is completed and each aspect of the young person's life is adequately considered.

Certain steps must be followed if young people are going to be able to participate fully in the planning process.

- It is important that the young person been consulted about the timing, date and venue of the review. It is essential that the young person is facilitated to attend a review if they so desire. Care experienced people often recall feeling stigmatised: e.g., by being withdrawn from school classes to attend reviews. They should be consulted about what works best for them, in their unique circumstances.
- Practitioners need to ensure that any particular needs the young person have are addressed. Young people should be enabled to participate in a way that suits them – they may want to communicate using the Makaton method of communication, e.g., or may want to use creative methods, such as providing a drawing or poem for the review to consider. The young person may require an advocate, who will ensure that their voice is heard and that their best interests are addressed.
- And the review should be organised in a young person-centred manner. Accessible language should be used, the venue should be appropriate and comfortable and the particular needs of the young person should be fully taken into account.

Sinclair (1998) in her research summarises four stages necessary for effectively involving young people in child care planning as follows:

- providing information
- consultation
- attending meetings, and
- receiving a record of decisions.

The issue of 'planning' the life of a young person also raises some interesting philosophical issues and challenges. Many reading this book will know that young people may not 'buy into' their plan and will resist their lives being planned by adults – be they parents or care professionals. In fact care careers, particularly for older young people, may be led by 'events' rather than 'plans'. For example, a young person may be re-united with a long-lost relative who offers to care for them, thus sometimes important changes can be brought about by chance events rather than from the impact of care planning. Enabling young people to play an active role in care planning, however, should help to boost their 'resilience' – their sense of control and influence over their own lives (see Williams, 2005).

Involving parents and carers in the planning process

As well as involving young people it is often important to involve their parents and carers in the planning and review process, depending on the exact nature of their situation. Again this will contribute to effective leaving care outcomes – if family and friendship networks are kept in place there will be a better chance of young people re-connecting with these networks once they have left formal care placements. The basic principles of care planning which we have already been discussed still apply: providing information, consultation, facilitating attendance at meetings and providing a record of decisions. We know from research that many young people will return to live with their family and therefore it is important if it at all possible to ensure that links with families are maintained and developed, as long as this is consistent with the best interests of the young person.

Towards effective care planning

The government Regulations (Department for Children, Schools and Families (2010a) provide a model for effective care planning particularly in ensuring that all children and young people in care must have a care plan. The regulations require that the care plan should be prepared before placement wherever this is possible, and if not possible within ten days after the commencement of the first placement. The plan should be agreed with the parent (or person with parental responsibility) if practicable.

The care plan consists of four elements: 'the plan for permanence'; 'the placement plan'; 'the health plan' and 'the personal education plan'.

The plan should address the following issues:

- family and social relationships
- emotional and behavioural developmental needs

- identity
- self-care skills
- name of the Independent Reviewing Officer
- the wishes and feelings of various people.

'The placement plan' must be prepared prior to placement, and if not reasonably practicable, within five working days of the placement commencing. It should be agreed with carers and signed by them. 'The placement plan' should set out how the placement will 'contribute to meeting [the young person's] needs', according to the Regulations.

Arguably the role of residential child care is underplayed in the 2010 Regulations (see paragraph 2.4, 2010a). However, the Regulations do pay some attention to the demands of working with older children in residential care settings:

> It is also important to think about the needs of older children and young people in relation to achieving permanence in their lives. They may not be able to live with birth parents for a variety of reasons nor wish to be in a foster home or to be adopted but prefer to live in a children's home. Nevertheless the care planning process must identify adults such as wider family and friends or other connected people who can provide emotional support and a long-term trusting relationship which will provide continuing support, particularly during periods of transition. Good quality work with families can help the young person build bridges back to his/her parents or other family members who may be able to provide that support even though it is not possible for the young person to live at home. (2010a, 2.6)

The role of the Independent Reviewing Officer

The Independent Reviewing Officer (IRO) is a central actor in relation to the care planning process and has a fundamental role to play. The 2010 Regulations set out the responsibilities of the IRO as follows:

> The IRO appointed for the child is responsible for monitoring the performance of the responsible authority functions in relation to the child's case. The intention is to enable the IRO to have an effective and independent oversight of the child's case to ensure that the care plan represents an effective response to the assessed needs of the child and that progress is being made towards achieving the identified outcomes (2010b, 2.17)

The role of the IRO is expanded further in a dedicated handbook: 'the aim is to give all looked after children the support and services that each requires, to enable them to reach their potential' (2010b, p. 4).

It is clear then that the IRO is central to planning for young people in care. The word 'independent' is crucial here – that IROs should be independent of case management in relation to the young person and, therefore, free to challenge policy and practice on behalf of the young person. They also require some independence within the wider local authority as they may need to challenge managerial decisions where necessary. Ultimately the IRO has the power to refer any cause for concern they have to CAFCASS (Children and Families Court Advisory and Support Services). The IRO Handbook explains that, 'One of the key functions of the IRO is to resolve problems arising out of the planning process' (2010b, p. 43).

Residential staff, foster carers and social workers may therefore find themselves being challenged by the IRO in terms of their decision-making in relation to the young person. An important role of the IRO is to make sure that decisions are followed through and that young people are not able to repeat a comment made during a 2001 study by Munro, 'they say they will talk about it at the next review but they never do' (2001, p. 131).

Young people's views of the role of the IRO

In 2011 the Children's Rights Director of Ofsted undertook a survey which examined the views of young people on the role of the IRO. 1530 young people responded, of which 17 per cent were in residential care. Of the young people who responded 79 per cent were aware that they had an IRO, and 71 per cent of this group knew how to contact their IRO. The majority of young people perceived the main roles of the IRO to be checking that the local authority was carrying on their role properly and to chair their reviews. About 500 young people could identify things that the IRO did well. The Ofsted report argues that this provides:

> strong support from children for how IROs are doing. Over half of the children who answered about what IROs needed to do better said there was nothing theirs needed to do better (2011b, p. 13).

The young people were also asked 'how many big decisions about their life are made in review meetings'? The answer from 59 per cent was that all or most important decisions are made in their reviews; 17 per cent replied that none were. Thirty per cent of young people said they needed someone apart from their social worker to undertake IRO tasks. One young person said that, 'social workers move on frequently, my IRO was around for 12 years' (2011b, p. 18), thus pointing to the need for some continuity in the lives of children and young people in care.

Young people were also asked about the need for IROs to be independent. Of the responses, 39 per cent said that they were happy for the local authority to employ the IRO and 29 per cent said they should be employed by more independent body.

This is important evidence about the key role of the IRO in ensuring effective care planning for young people.

'Leaving care' and the 'transition to adulthood'

We have seen here that planning for leaving care is clearly an important element of the care experience. Again the English regulations provide a potential model for planning the transition to adulthood process. The Regulations argue that:

> Research and practice shows that young people who have been looked after will have the best chance of success as adults if those providing transitional care and other support take the following principles into account in talking to the young person and when making any decision:

- 'Is this good enough for my own child?
- [Are we] providing a second chance if things don't go as expected?
- Is this tailored to their individual needs, particularly if they are more vulnerable than other young people?' (Department for Education, 2010, p. 4)

As we have seen, the central plan for a young person leaving care in this system is known as the 'pathway plan', which must be designed for each child and young person. It should be prepared before they leave care and should be considered and revised at reviews following the process we have already outlined, under the guidance of an IRO.

The expectations of the social worker in relation to the young person are clearly established within the Guidance, with the following people being consulted in relation to planning for the young person:

- ... the young person's parents, other adults with parental responsibility and relevant members of their wider family network;
- the young person's current carer and any prospective future provider of housing and accommodation support;

- the young person's designated teacher, college tutor or other educational professional familiar with the young person's learning needs and educational objectives;
- any independent visitor appointed for the young person;
- a designated nurse for looked after children or any other medical professional providing health care or treatment named in their health plan;
- any PA (personal adviser), already appointed to support the young person;
- the young person's IRO; and
- any advocate acting for the young person' (Department for Education, 2010, p. 15)

The exact nature of any consultation will of course vary according to the young person's particular situation and their wishes and feelings about who should be involved. The Guidance also places a strong emphasis on the views of the young person and how these should be recorded:

The views of the young person must be recorded and incorporated into the pathway plan. The plan must also indicate how arrangements to support the young person have taken the views of the others listed above into account. Disagreements between the young person and professionals should be noted carefully. (Department for Education, 2010, p. 15).

The pathway plan for the young person should cover the following issues:

... the young person's health and development building on the information included in the young person's health plan established within their care plan when they were looked after. The plan should support the young person's access to positive activities, education, training and employment. The Personal Education Plan (PEP) should continue to be maintained while the young person continues to receive full or part-time education. Information within the PEP will feed directly into the Pathway Plan. Pathway plans must have an explicit focus on career planning, taking into account the young person's aspirations, skills, and educational potential, contact with the young person's parents, wider family and friends and the capacity of this network to encourage the young person and enable them to make a positive transition to adulthood, the young person's financial capabilities and money management capacity, along with strategies to develop the young person's skills in this area. (Department for Education, 2010, pp. 13–14).

We can see that care planning for young people 'leaving care' shares many characteristics with care planning in general, but self-evidently, with a strong focus on the transition to adulthood.

Young people's views of the role of care planning and leaving care

Munro *et al.* evaluated the 'Right2BCared4' pilots which looked as part of the study at care planning, and focused on preparation for leaving care and how this could be improved. In summary the study, which included young people in a variety of care settings, found that:

- 'The majority of young people felt 'very' or 'quite' involved in the preparation of their pathway plan.
- Young people valued plans that explored how their current circumstances might change, when goals were set and when it was clear what services the local authority would supply to support them in making the transition to adulthood.
- Young people reported that delays in completion of plans, or failure to review and update them, undermined their relevance.
- Most young people reported that they were always encouraged to express their wishes and feelings at review meetings: however, only 53 per cent felt they were always listened to.
- Around two-thirds of young people were in favour of additional reviews when significant changes were proposed ... findings from interviews revealed that the review meeting itself could inhibit their active participation if it involved a large number of professionals' (Munro *et al.*, 2011, p. x)

Here we can see that elements of the care planning process are working well but there remains considerable room for improvement.

Support after leaving care

In recent years we have witnessed a shift away from the concept of 'leaving care' towards that of 'transition to adulthood'. Whilst this may seem like mere semantics, it is underpinned by some important shifts in policy and practice.

The issue of young people leaving the care of the local authority became a high-profile issue during the 1980s following pressure brought about young people and their organisations and the publication of the key text, *Leaving Care* (Stein and Carey, 1986). Young people leaving care have been seen by successive British governments as being vulnerable to a number of indicators of social inequality, for example:

In the year ending 31 March 2001 37 per cent of care leavers obtained one or more GCSE or GNVQ compared to 94 per cent of Year 11 pupils in England as a whole ...

Unemployment amongst care leavers was around 50 per cent compared to 19 per cent of young people in the country at the time of the survey ...

One-in-seven young women leaving care were pregnant or young mothers. (*Action on Aftercare*, 2004, p. 2).

Research suggests that, in terms of employability, the age at which a young person leaves care is very significant, with those leaving after 18 being much more likely to hold down a job: 73 per cent are economically active nine to 10 months after leaving care, compared to 33 per cent of those who left at 16, and 32 per cent of those who left at 17 (Action for Children, 2011, p. 17).

It can be seen that much remains to be done in terms of improving outcomes for children leaving care. Stein, a leading British researcher in this area, argues that we can usefully see the care-leaving population as falling into three groups (see Action on Aftercare, 2004, p. 4).

1   (The most successful group), a 'moving on' group: young people who have usually experienced stability in care, and as a result are highly resilient. This group often welcomes opportunities offered for greater independence on the journey to adulthood. They often achieve successful outcomes.

2   A 'survivors' group. This group may have experienced more instability and change whilst in the care system than the 'moving on' group. In order to achieve more positive outcomes these young people are more dependent on the type of aftercare support that they receive. The role of leaving care services will be central if they too are to achieve successful outcomes.

3   A more vulnerable 'victims' group including young people who have experienced the most damaging pre-care experiences. The care system was unable to compensate for these and they may well have experienced change and disruption whilst in care. They required more careful and consistent support whilst in care. Aftercare support is very important to them but is unlikely to be able to compensate for their negative experiences before or during care. This leaves them vulnerable and they may struggle to achieve positive outcomes.

In their assessment of the impact of English Children (Leaving Care) Act 2000, the Action on After Care consortium argued that the successes and any concerns about the Act can be classified as follows, in four categories:

Resources: it would seem that more resources have been dedicated to leaving care services and that as a result there are more workers with specialist skills in the leaving care area. There are concerns that the increase in resources might not be sustainable in the long run and with particular concerns around leisure and housing.

Roles, responsibilities and strategic planning: there seem to have been improvements in strategic planning, clearer policies and clearer views of roles and responsibilities. Concerns are mainly focused around the needs of particular groups of young people: e.g., young people leaving custody, unaccompanied asylum seeking children, and young people with complex needs and young parents.

Outcomes: the report found some limited improvement in outcomes (given the relatively short period since the Act had been implemented). Concerns focused around methods for measuring outcomes which we return to below.

Young people's experience: seemed to have improved in terms of the increased focus on support and planning in the Act. There were still concerns about income levels and clarity in terms of rights and entitlements.

(Action on Aftercare, 2004, pp. 6–9).

As can be seen from this evidence leaving care remains a complex and challenging area for policymakers and practitioners alike.

Stein concludes that we need a progress measure that measures the journey of young people whilst they have been in the care system. He argues that this method would be would be more realistic than the 'sad litany of poor outcomes' utilised by many commentators on the care system. Stein argues that we also need to see young peoples' problems more in the context of wider social challenges – such as poverty, family problems and poor education. It is unrealistic to expect the care system to compensate for wider social problems and challenges, as if it existed in isolation from fundamental social and structural forces.

One important message from all the research and statistics explored in this chapter is that the experience of leaving care should be seen as a process not an event. The importance of seeing leaving care as an extended process is highlighted in this way in the report:

For young people who have been in care, the expectation that most will be living independently by 16 is also out of step with what happens to other young people, most of whom are now staying in the family home until their mid-twenties or even later. Many care leavers in our interviews said they felt this abrupt end to their time in care was a shock. One said: 'You haven't got the sense of security you used to have with your foster placement. You used to be able to just go home and have your food on the table and your washing would be done, but now you've got to do it all yourself. It's alright to do it yourself, but it can be a struggle' (Action for Children, 2011, p. 17).

In summary the extensive research on leaving care suggests that a successful transition to adulthood for young care leavers involves the following:

- Choosing when to leave care
- Being prepared emotionally
- Being supported by leaving care services, family, friends and mentors
- Having an income or receiving enough financial assistance
- Being involved in decisions. (Centre for Excellence and Outcomes, 2010b, p. 24)

Having conducted a review of the leaving care research the voluntary organisation Action for Children concludes as follows in relation to the reforms required to improve the experience of young people leaving care:

- Promoting a successful transition to adulthood is about supporting young people to develop the life skills required in later life. Key to this process is providing flexible support to young people as they, inevitably, make mistakes, and being there to help them draw lessons from their experiences.
- Young people leaving institutional care, including the secure estate, must be confident that the resources are there to support successful resettlement into the community. Inadequate accommodation and housing support for care leavers and young ex-offenders places them a real risk of homelessness, unemployment, and ultimately offending.
- A child-fair state is one that ensures all children and young people can access the support they need to move into adulthood. Where structural obstacles and financial disincentives prevent young people from moving into employment and training programmes, these need to be removed so that all young people can achieve economic success.
- Employability and training services outside of school are essential for the most disaffected young people to develop aspirations and plan for the future. Working with this group of young people requires time and patience. Government must recognise the need for programmes that develop a young person's ability to learn, and that focus on achievement and progress made, not simply educational attainment and gaining qualifications. (Action for Children, 2011, p. 23)

What makes the difference?: an important research project

One significant achievement within the care system in recent years has been the way that young people have become more active participants in planning and policy development around the care system (see Stein, 2011). The shift towards active participation has also been demonstrated in research: and thus it is worth examining in some detail a powerful example of peer research in relation to leaving care.

The 'What Makes the Difference' (WMTD) project was a European Community funded project which funded young person peer research on the transition to adulthood for care experienced young people. The study provides an important insight into the experiences of young people leaving care in England. The report argues that outcomes for care leavers in employment, education, housing and health demonstrate 'significant failings in the preparation and readiness of looked after children and care leavers for adult life' (WMTD, 2008). The WMTD peer research demonstrated that '38 per cent of young people with care experience believe they are simply left to "get on with it" without any input or preparation when the time came to live independently' (WMTD, 2008).

The sudden nature of transition without adequate support is illustrated by one young person in these words:

> I moved into supported housing at 18 and had to learn how to stand on my own two feet very quickly. I didn't have any support and suddenly had to fill in housing applications and learn how to budget (WMTD, 2008).

As we have seen, young people leaving care tend to experience independent living earlier than the remainder of the population:

> This lack of preparation is even more significant when you consider the fact that young people leaving care face independence far earlier than their peers. While the average young person now leaves home at 24 – and will usually go safe in the knowledge that they can call on their parents for advice and support, the majority of care leavers move to independent living well before their 18th birthday and don't have anyone to fall back on. They need to learn how to budget, deal with emergencies, cook, clean, and much, much more without having a mum or dad to call on for advice and help. (WMTD, 2008)

The WMTD report provides a blueprint for what needs to improve if outcomes for young people are to improve; its suggestions are worthy of detailed attention.

The report initially addresses issues of preparation and planning:

- 'Pathway planning and preparation is still inadequate for many young people and a significant number have to leave care before they are ready.
- Our peer research findings showed that 23 per cent of interviewees didn't have or weren't sure if they had a pathway plan. 49 per cent received no written information about entitlements when they leave care.
- Preparation work needs to start from as early as possible, well before pathway planning to ensure enough time for young people to practice and develop the necessary life skills.
- Our peer research findings showed that 37 per cent of interviewees thought that advice on leaving care should be given at aged 16 or under.
- 43 per cent of those interviewed believed financial advice was key to their ability to live independently, ahead of emotional support which was identified by 26 per cent.
- Financial help and advice on housing, employment and cooking are also identified as important factors.' (WMTD, 2008)

The report then goes on to argue that preparation needs to start as early as possible, and that it must reflect the ability of the young person:

- 'There is a need for preparation work to start from as early as possible to ensure enough time for young people to practice and develop the necessary life skills.
- Our peer research findings showed that 37 per cent of interviewees thought that advice on leaving care should be given at aged 16 or under.
- However, when to start must be dependent upon age and ability and vulnerability rather than being driven by the need to ensure young people leave care at 16/17 years old.
- The fear and anxiety implicit within the current system undermines young people's ability and opportunity for success.
- For all young people learning about adult life must be experiential, so that they can test out their skills as they move towards independence.
- The process must be well planned, as safe as possible and at a pace that young people can cope with – and most importantly it must have a "safety net" attached'. (WMTD, 2008)

The WMTD report also reinforces our earlier point that young people must be fully involved in the process:

- 'It is important to recognise that young people are experts when it comes to the care system.
- Including their feedback as service users is the only way to make effective improvements to services.
- If we are to improve outcomes for young people in and from care it is important to involve those young people in training the people who provide the services.
- As we found in our pilot, training young people to deliver the training is very effective and beneficial for both young people, who gain valuable experience and to learn and develop new skills, and for workers who benefit from hearing what young people think and want'. (WMTD, 2008)

Here we have a blueprint for the future of leaving care, literally from the voices of young people themselves. We certainly seem to have sufficient knowledge about how to transform the care system to improve outcomes for young people – but it remains a significant challenge for the system to actually deliver these outcomes. Given that we have this extensive knowledge of the challenges facing young people leaving the care system and at least an idea about 'what works' to improve the situation, what should happen next? In 2012 a consortium of 'leaving care' organisations made a powerful case for change to the British government. In a report entitled 'Access all Areas' they made an 'overarching recommendation':

> ... for central government departments to make a commitment to 'care-proof' all government policies by assessing the impact they will have on looked after children and care leavers and those who support them. This work should be co-ordinated and monitored through the establishment of a cross-departmental working group to consider care leaver issues in broader government policy, with a view to producing an associated action plan for each department. (National Care Advisory Service and others, 2012, p. 3).

Building on research such as that explored elsewhere in this chapter the report argues that:

> Evidence has shown that leaving care services are able to provide the best services where they have good working relationships with external health, accommodation and education, training and employment

agencies and there is specialist provision providing careers advice, negotiating suitable accommodation and addressing health and wellbeing needs. To ensure this happens central government needs to ensure the necessary legislation, regulation and guidance is in place and is consistently implemented. (National Care Advisory Service and others, 2012, p. 6)

The 'Access All Areas' report provides a blueprint that presents a way forward for making a fundamental change for young people leaving the care system.

Conclusion

Leaving care, as we have seen, is in many ways the acid test of the care system. In this chapter we have explored the three key elements of the process: the impact of the care experience itself; support in moving towards the transition to adulthood; and the experience of young people once they have left care.

We have seen that in many ways we know 'what works' for young people leaving care. We have seen these messages reinforced by peer research by young people. The research is extensive and in many respects (in England, for example), the legal and regulatory framework is already in place. We now need a step-change to ensure that the experience of leaving care is a consistent one for young people and that they are fully supported in the transition to adulthood – particularly as that transition is becoming more difficult for all young people, regardless of whether they are care experienced or not.

7 Being in care: a global experience
A global perspective

> I had so many [placements] that I can't give a significant number. You
> get moved around a lot …When you have been in care in a way you are
> lucky because you have lived all over so you can say I love this place
> and hate that place – so in that way we are lucky.
>
> (Zac, in care in1990s and 2000s)

All cultures, historically and geographically, have had systems for coping
with those children and young people unable to live with their birth families
(Hendrick, 2003). These systems have sometimes been uncaring and
heartless: even encompassing the extreme of infanticide as a method of
removing unwanted children. From the 1700s onwards children were cared
for in institutions – such as the foundling hospitals established in great cities
such as Florence, London and Paris. The Victorian philanthropists – like
Doctor Thomas Barnardo – began to form elaborate systems of care
involving residential care, fostering and sometimes the migration of children
to far-away countries (Bean and Melville, 1990). Today care systems are
diverse and disparate – reflecting the separate histories and cultures of each
nation around the world.

Without being able to go into too much detail, this chapter examines
some key challenges faced in those diverse systems. We explore the
different care concepts found around the world, the usefulness of the
'social pedagogue' as a cross-border initiative and an actual transnational
case study.

Concepts and approaches

Many challenges face those studying the different care systems found across
the globe. A fundamental difficulty is posed by the fact that different
language and concepts are used to describe and understand young people in
the care system or leaving care and the carers that work with them.

Thoburn and Courtney (2011) provide a useful discussion of how the language of child welfare differs across the globe. In the United States for example, 'foster care' refers to:

> ... all types of publically-provided child welfare placements, including what in other countries is referred to as 'group care', 'residential care', 'children's homes' or 'institutional care. (2011, p. 211).

They go on to explain that in the United States 'family foster care' is what in the United Kingdom would be referred to simply as 'foster care', which would often be with strangers.

These linguistic differences reflect important organisational differences – for example some countries provide largely state-based care; others faith-based care and yet others care delivered largely through NGOs. Global care systems vary considerably – both in terms of how they are organised and how they are conceptualised and understood.

The scale of the challenge of caring for separated young people will differ considerably – say between industrialised Western societies compared with developing countries. In England for example there are now children's homes that care for as few as one, two or three children: this can be compared with large-scale orphanages that care for many hundreds of children in a country such as India. For example, one international study of 12 nation states points out that:

> The percentage of young people living in large residential care facilities in the countries under review varied between 4 per cent in Albania and 98 per cent in Bulgaria (Lerch and Stein, 2010, p. 130).

We can see that the nature of the care population and the challenges of caring for them will vary considerably in these differing contexts.

As well as these differences, however, there are a considerable number of shared issues including:

- How can admission to care be avoided?
- Which system works most effectively for children and young people?
- How can young people be best supported in leaving care?

Munro and colleagues (2011) utilise the United Nations Convention on the Rights of the Child (UNHRC) to provide a global perspective on young people in the care system, in order to assess if there is a common thread in addressing the global challenge of caring for children in state care.

Those authors point to a key development of the 1960s and 1970s in the Western world, namely a shift away from the provision of large-scale institutional care. As we saw in Chapter 3 this was led by a number of factors including influential radical anti-institutional thought (by authors such as Erving Goffman and R. D. Laing), and pro-family approaches which favoured 'family-based' care , such as adoption and fostering. At various points and times across the globe, however, there have been arguments for returning to institutional care. For example, Allen and Varca (2011), use the oft-quoted poor outcomes in relation to foster care to argue for a return to what they refer to as 'orphanages'. The authors quote the US Executive Director of Children's Rights as stating that foster care in the United States 'is a system that is producing very bad results for kids' (Allen and Varca, 2011, p. 1067). They blame many of these failures on changes in placements which in turn lead to changes of school: 'Most of these children move from school to school because they frequently change foster homes' (2011, p. 1068).

In order to address these shortcomings Allen and Varca critically examine arguments for a return to more extensive provision of residential care (see Smith (1996) for a historical perspective on this debate). A similar case is made by McKenzie (1999) in his 'Re-thinking Orphanages for the 21st Century' where he argues that: 'the evidence is mounting that children's homes have worked well in past, are working well now, and can work even better in the future' (1999, p. 308).

Allen and Varca provide brief case studies of four residential settings in order to explore potential options.

1 They explore the Milton Hershey School, a campus with small houses where young people live with house parents and is quoted as producing positive educational outcomes.
2 They look at the Boys Town in Nebraska, which is described as providing, 'a residential family atmosphere for boys and girls that have been abused and neglected by their parents' (2011, p. 1069). The authors argue that destinations for young people leaving Boys Town are much more positive than those for young people ageing out of foster care.
3 Drawing on a system rather than a single example, they outline the Kinderhaus German system, which has been widely identified as providing positive experiences and outcomes for children and young people.

Allen and Varca relate the success of this system to the role of the 'social pedagogue'. Finally, the authors refer to the work of the SEED foundation which combines a strong focus on education with a 'nurturing residential program' (2011, p. 1070). Overall the authors conclude that, 'the time has come to incorporate the success of the four programs reviewed and embrace them as a pathway to provide a better ... care system for our youth' (2011, p. 1070).

Social pedagogy can be defined as follows:

> The basic idea of social pedagogy is to promote people's social functioning, inclusion, participation, social identity and social competence as members of society. Its particular terms of reference apply to the problems people have in integration and life phases of the lifespan (Hamalanen in Berridge *et al.*, 2011, p. 4).

Petrie *et al.* undertook fieldwork in Belgium, Denmark, France, Germany and the Netherlands for a study of the role and they describe pedagogy as, 'education in its broadest sense' and as 'bringing up children in a way that addresses the whole child' (2006, p. 20).

The key principles of pedagogy can be outlined as follows according to Berridge and colleagues:

- focus on the child as a whole person
- practitioners see themselves as a person and use individual attributes and skills in the relationship with the child
- children and staff occupy the same life-space, not separate hierarchical domains
- pedagogues adopt a reflexive approach to their practice and apply theoretical understanding and self-knowledge to their relationships
- practical skills are important and pedagogues became involved in children's daily lives and activities
- the group is a useful resource
- there is a genuine interest in children's rights beyond narrow legal and procedural requirements
- teamwork is important: with parents, other professionals and the local community.
- The relationship is central, together with the importance of listening and communicating (Berridge *et al.*, 2011, p. 22)

It is important that social pedagogy should not be seen simply as a 'technique', rather as an approach embedded in a social philosophy and a social context. As we have seen throughout this book the structure and design of each care system is closely related to the social history, politics and values of the specific nation state. Thus, for example, England has comparatively fine a lower number of children in care than most other European countries – leading to children in care having more severe challenges in their lives and, perhaps as a result, poorer outcomes (Thoburn, 2008). By contrast, residential accommodation tends to be used more extensively in some European countries, including Germany, for example.

Often there is a flexible boundary between living with a birth family and being in the care system. Education on the same site as the care premises is also used more frequently in many European countries than in England where the model on 'community home (education)', popular in the post-Second World War period, has been largely discontinued.

The influence of European models of provision for children in care was reflected in the decision by the British New Labour government to pilot social pedagogy as an approach in England. The pilot was undertaken as part of an extensive reform programme known as 'Care Matters' (see Frost and Parton, 2009) and the outcomes of the pilot are reported by Berridge *et al.* (2011) who undertook the official evaluation.

Building on the Thomas Coram Research Unit influential research project mentioned above (Petrie *et al.*, 2006) the Department of Children, Schools and Families provided resources to recruit social pedagogues from Denmark, Germany, Flanders and Belgium to work in England. The programme was funded for two years and the pedagogues were allocated to four groups to facilitate effective evaluation. These groups were as follows:

- *Group 1*: four homes where social pedagogues (SPs) had worked prior to the scheme (homes that had had the experience of pedagogues working with them, and were continuing to work with them).
- *Group 2*: eight single home sites where social pedagogues were employed.
- *Group 3*: six sites that combined direct work and local consultancy.
- *Group 4*: 12 homes to provide a research comparison group – where social pedagogues were not employed and had never been employed.

The Berridge *et al.* study undertook a sophisticated and extensive approach to studying the role of the social pedagogue in the English context. Outcomes for young people were assessed using a number of measures including:

> ... some standardised measures as well as quantitative and qualitative assessments of: behavioural and emotional factors; violent behaviour; delinquency; risk behaviour and self-harm; going missing; educational involvement and attainment; and family contact. (Berridge *et al.*, pp. 252–3)

The findings in relation to outcomes are however arguably disappointing:

- There was considerable turnover in the population of residents of the homes, with 43–66 per cent of residents making (planned or unplanned) moves during each of the three study periods. It is therefore difficult to be sure whether any changes over time were due to the introduction of social pedagogy or due to the substantial fluctuation in the population of the homes.

- The only significant change in outcomes over time occurred in relation to placement disruption, which decreased significantly during the period six months before the SPs joined the homes to one year after the first SP was employed.
- With the exception of rates of temporary exclusion from school, there were no significant differences in outcomes between the pilot and comparison homes.
- The residents of some, but not all, of the homes became involved in the criminal justice system and were excluded from school. This may have been affected by differences in home population, or peer or staff cultures, or a mixture of these. (Berridge *et al.*, pp. 246–7)

The evaluation team placed their findings in a social and policy context:

The Social Pedagogues [from around Europe] were ... rather taken aback by the role of the residential worker in England. They had a range of professional qualifications, the majority of them graduates, and some were also equipped to be employed as social workers in their own country or to work with other user groups as well in a range of other responsible roles. In contrast, in children's residential care, their English equivalents have low status and little influence. Their professional input is marginalised and they lack autonomy. They usually refer on to experts rather than take control of issues themselves. English homes have fewer residents than elsewhere but with many more staff, who work in a hierarchical setting. England has little residential care and a heterogeneous mix. Young people tend not to stay for long. Our child care system is over-bureaucratic and risk-averse. History and policy have created this set of circumstances or not altered them. It is unsurprising that our continental visitors often felt bemused and deskilled (2011, p. 252).

Berridge *et al.* conclude their study as follows:

... there were no significant differences in outcomes between homes in Groups 1–3 and Group 4, or between the four groups individually. In other words, pilot homes which employed SPs made no more progress with residents' wellbeing than did those without (2011, p. 253).

Whilst one can detect the disappointment of the research team in their own findings, these need to be placed in a wider context:

Even within the constraints of this exercise, it is disappointing that homes – with or without SPs – were not making marked progress with groups of residents but we should not rush to judgement. We have seen that homes accommodate very problematic youngsters, mainly for planned, brief periods. They usually arrive at a late stage with problems entrenched. There is restricted time to influence these established patterns and to develop positive influence. Homes are open environments, mostly close to family, friends and communities, all of which exert influence alongside what the residential home has to offer (2011, p. 253).

More optimistically the Berridge team argue that:

There were certainly features of the social pedagogy philosophy which seemed valuable. Overall it provides coherence and meaning to residential life to which staff can subscribe; otherwise homes can be anomic and staff inconsistent. Most pilot homes that we visited seemed to have some overarching theoretical underpinning but about a third did not. Young people's behaviour and responses can be very menacing for staff in the absence of a conceptual framework to understand and respond. Indeed, SPs often referred to child development and other theories in their work, which would be more unusual for the English workforce (2011, p. 256).

They also argue that:

The social pedagogic distinction between 'the professional, personal and private' also seemed to us useful. SPs were sometimes prepared to share more about themselves personally (*not* private details), which felt more caring, genuine and potentially empowering. Young people could see that staff themselves had experienced – and often overcome – problems, as well as having their own limitations and faults. This feels a stronger basis to establish relationships in daily living than adopting one-sided, professional detachment. In addition, skilled SPs that we encountered prioritised project work and shared activities ('common third'). This had a therapeutic purpose and often involved embarking together on a joint, new activity. It opened-up the opportunity for shared space and discussion (2011, p. 256).

The authors are forced to conclude that the relative lack of measurable impact of the pilot is not linked to various technical aspects of the pilot (its short-term nature, e.g.) but more broadly to the social, political and cultural factors discussed throughout this book. They point out that: 'social work in England (and the USA) traditionally have an 'individualist' approach compared with more collectivist or 'reflexive-therapeutic' styles in other countries' (2011, p. 256).

Cross-continental comparisons

The non-governmental organisation SOS Children's Villages has published a study of 'ageing out of care' in 2010 which gives us one of the few truly multi-national studies of care systems. The study includes data from countries where SOS Children's Villages has projects and includes the following nations:

- Azerbaijan
- Bosnia and Herzegovina
- Bulgaria
- Croatia
- Czech Republic
- Estonia
- France
- Georgia
- Kyrgyzstan
- Poland
- Russian Federation and
- Uzbekistan.

The researchers argue that having gathered data from these 12 countries:

> ... recurring themes emerge across national boundaries, highlighting the importance of de-institutionalisation efforts, national standards and the dissemination of good practice. (Lerch and Stein, 2010, p. 7).

The following shared themes are used to analyse the findings from the 12 nations:

- preparation
- housing
- employment
- coverage gaps
- emotional hardship
- abuse
- inefficiency in the care system
- uneven provision and legal gaps

The report argues having considered all these issues that in general 'young people are not sufficiently prepared for leaving care' (2010, p. 7) and they argue that lack of preparation is strongly associated with institutionalisation, which is extensively utilised in some of the nations studied: 'the most common theme identified in the 12 country chapters can be captured by the term institutionalisation' (Lerch and Stein, 2010, p. 132).

There were shared problems with access to adequate housing for young people leaving care across the 12 countries. For example:

> In Albania, where access to residential care ends once a young person turns 15, most care leavers become homeless – and thus more exposed to violence, sexual abuse and trafficking. (2010, p. 7)

The report explains that, 'care leavers speak of the incapacitating impact of loneliness, emptiness and abandonment' (Lerch and Stein, 2010, p. 7). This is an emotional and hard-hitting perception of the potential negative impact of being unable to remain with one's birth family.

As one would expect across 12 nations there is also considerable national variation. In Azebiajan, for example, 'girls are at high risk of being physically and sexually abused by staff and peers' (Lerch and Stein, 2010, p. 7).

As we saw in Chapter 6:

> International evidence suggests ... that, as a group, young people leaving care are more disadvantaged and face more difficulties than other young people ... their journey to adulthood is shorter, more severe, and often more hazardous (Lerch and Stein, 2010, p. 129).

We can see how nation states vary in their approach to children and young people in care, for example, in the age of leaving care: 'official statistics from the eight countries that did provide information reveal that the age of care leavers ranges from 15 to 26 years of age'. (Lerch and Stein, 2010, p. 130)

The impact of large-scale institutionalisation is also apparent in the study: 'In eight of the twelve countries, data reveals that young people who leave large residential care facilities encounter the most difficulties' (Lerch and Stein, 2010, p. 131).

The authors point to some of the causes of poor outcomes for children and young people in the care system, and also to some of the positives. They argue that:

> ... fragmentation of responsibilities has a negative impact on the quality of child care services. The implementation of the legislation

and the provision of children's services could be split between central and local government. In all country chapters, the involvement of NGOs in the provision of services was seen as positive. (Lerch and Stein, 2010, p. 131)

They also argue from a strong and unified legislative approach to leaving care:

... very little legislation specifically addresses the preparation for leaving care or support for young care leavers. Legal provisions are contained within more general social care or child care legislation (Lerch and Stein, 2010, p. 131)

The international evidence almost inevitably points to uneven approaches:

In all 12 countries, 'preparation programmes' are being carried out: however, evidence shows that access to such programmes and the quality of preparation vary greatly within and across countries, suggesting that not all young people are adequately prepared for adulthood (Lerch and Stein, 2010, p. 132).

The research also points to a shortfall in the types of provision and support offered to young people in care and ageing out of care:

... little evidence of young care leavers being offered skilled counselling to help them overcome the often persistent psychological problems caused by institutionalisation, including a sense of isolation, difficulties in forming relationships, and more problems regarding the general social integration into their communities (Lerch and Stein, 2010, p. 132)

In conclusion the study makes an over-arching recommendation for all 12 countries:

... establishing a new legal framework specifically for preparation and after-care services or strengthening the existing law; and drawing up a national strategy and clear standards for preparation and after-care services (Lerch and Stein, 2010, p. 133).

In terms of law, policy and practice the report recommends:

... improving interdepartmental coordination at the national level; reducing the fragmentation of responsibilities among government departments; and enhancing local government interagency cooperation, including the involvement of NGOs. (Lerch and Stein, 2010, p. 133)

These recommendations are consistent with those explored in Chapter 6. The authors also suggest that there is a need for standards and benchmarking, such as those outlined in the British government guidance explored earlier in this book:

> Most (country) chapters specifically call for the implementation of quality standards that comply with the United Nations Guidelines for the Alternative Care of Children and the Quality4Children standards to improve the quality of care, preparation, and after-care services. (Lerch and Stein, 2010, p. 133)

Further cross-national recommendations are made which include the following:

- working with families to prevent young people from being placed in alternative care;
- administering additional training, including for 'guardians', carers, and staff;
- systematically collecting more reliable official data;
- monitoring care leavers based on indicators such as education, employment, training, accommodation, health and wellbeing;
- conducting research into problems of and services available to young people leaving care;
- deinstitutionalising care by shifting placement to family settings such as foster care and smaller children's homes;
- enhancing links between young people and their families of origin;
- expanding the range and comprehensiveness of preparation and after-care services (such as housing and employment priority schemes; financial assistance; personal support; and crisis services);
- redoubling involvement with NGOs;
- encouraging greater involvement of young people in the development of preparation and after-care services;
- developing care leavers' own support networks and related websites;
- and increasing public awareness of the problems and challenges faced by young people leaving care. (Lerch and Stein, 2010, pp. 133–4)

We can see from this innovative study that whilst there are important differences between care systems there are also elements in common where shared and common reforms can help improve the quality of life of young people 'ageing out of care'.

Conclusion

This chapter has allowed us to provide a brief overview of some of the issues that arise from a global perspective on care systems. Unsurprisingly we find that there are both many shared issues and challenges and many points of difference between nation states. In our concluding chapter we share some suggestions for improving the lives of young people involved in the care system.

8   Promoting positive outcomes for children and young people in care

Health and education

> (The social worker) came with me to my interview at uni and when they said I didn't have enough UCAS points he asked if he could have a word. I don't know what he said but I got into uni then! I'm still in contact with him now, he really went the extra mile … .
>
> (Clare, in care, late 1990s and 2000s)

As we have seen throughout this book children in care face many challenges in their lives, which often ad an extra dimension to the day-to-day issues faced by other children and young people. A fundamental function for all the professionals working with children and young people in care is to address the health and educational inequalities that they face. These young people will often start from a position of disadvantage in relation to health and education related to their pre-care experiences. It is important that the care system redresses these disadvantages so that young people do not accumulate disadvantage during their time in care.

Health needs of children and young people in care

As Scott and Ward accurately state:

> Despite the efforts of policy-makers and professionals, meeting the health needs of children and young people in care continues to be a challenge and it is likely that a series of factors are acting in combination as unwitting barriers to meeting their needs. (2008, p. 37)

As with many of the issues raised in this book taking action involves working together with a wide range of professionals, the young person's carers, parents and, of course, the young people themselves. Health is of central importance for all of us: being healthy underpins all other issues; a person who is not healthy will often experience disadvantage in all other aspects of their lives.

One key theme of this study has been to recognise the strengths of young people in care and point out that it is important not to see such young people simply as 'problematic' or 'troubled'. For example, in relation to health, carers assess the health of children and young people in care to be good or very good for about two-thirds of the care population (Meltzer *et al.* 2003). Having noted this, it is nevertheless the case that if care-experienced young people leave care with their health needs unaddressed they will carry these health inequalities with them into the rest of their lives.

All professional work in England with looked after children is underpinned by the Guidance published under the Children Act 1989 – guidance that was reviewed and re-issued in 2010 – and the 'Statutory Guidance on promoting the health and wellbeing of Looked After Children', published in 2009. These publications act as a guide to good practice and are transferable to differing national contexts.

Health challenges for looked after children

The health inequalities faced by looked-after young people are fundamentally rooted in three main factors. First, children in care are more likely to be from a background of poverty and disadvantage than other young people (Bebbington and Miles, 1989) and we also know from research that poorer children suffer disproportionately from health inequalities (see Acheson, 1998, and Wilkinson and Pickett, 2010, e.g.).

Second the majority, although we should note, not all, children and young people in care will have had specific experiences that led to them to being looked after that have an impact on their health and wellbeing. Some may have even had experience in the womb if their mother was using drugs or alcohol. They may also have been abused or neglected and this experience could also contribute to them experiencing health and developmental disadvantage (Turney & Tanner, 2003).

Third, as with many of the other issues addressed in this book, health disadvantage may be compounded or may accumulate if a young person experiences changes in placement or if professional practice does not fully address their needs.

In summary – children in care may have experienced health inequalities before coming into care grounded in a number of factors and effective multi-professional working is required if these inequalities are to be effectively addressed.

What would effective professional practice look like if we are to improve health outcomes for children and young people in care?

First, we need to work towards stability of placement for those young people – which is strongly associated with improvements in health.

Second, it is important to ensure that professional practice is high quality and that professional staff work together to promote positive health outcomes for children in care.

Third, professionals need to make sure that foster and residential carers are prepared and are well-informed in order to effectively promote the health of the children and young people that they care for.

Fourth, and finally, we should remember that young people sometimes involve themselves in activities which may actively undermine their health – including for example substance abuse or potentially harmful sexual activities – and we need to do everything possible to reduce these harmful activities.

The National Children's Bureau (2008), based in London, reflect such good practice in their National Healthy Care Standard. The standard is based on a child and young person's entitlement to the following:

- appreciation, love, respect and consistency
- a safe, protective and healthy care environment
- opportunities to develop personal and social skills to enable them to care for their health and wellbeing now and in the future
- effective healthcare, assessment, treatment and support (www.ncb.org. uk/healthycare).

The challenge of addressing the health needs of children in care is considerable, covering topics including the following:

- working in partnership with young person
- assessing needs and gathering relevant information
- multi-professional practice
- providing stability in high quality placements
- taking appropriate action following effective assessment.

Each of these professional responsibilities are discussed below. The discussion draws on legislation, guidance and research literature.

Working with the young person in care

Understanding health needs of young people in care requires a comprehensive and holistic approach. A comprehensive approach to health involves promoting the physical, emotional and sexual health of a young person, and this in turn is closely related to self-esteem and resilience. When young people themselves have been asked about health they favour a holistic approach within a broad definition of their health needs. Saunders and Broad

(1997) asked young people leaving care what the five most important factors affecting their health were. The young people replied as follows:

- feelings about life (71 per cent)
- housing (60 per cent)
- close personal relationships (56 per cent)
- care experience (42 per cent)
- depression (42 per cent).

The factors identified relate to a holistic, social approach with more predictable health concerns, such as smoking and diet, appearing lower down the list.

Government Statutory Guidance also quotes research illustrating young people's perspectives on their health care needs:

- more than a third of the young people felt that their health was only average;
- a large number felt that they were [experiencing] or had experienced stress;
- cost was seen as a barrier when considering healthy eating;
- very few people chose to go to professionals when considering sexual health;
- young people in care seek support from family and friends they left behind;
- peer pressure is a big impact on lifestyle choice for young people. (2009, p. 17)

In order to work effectively we need to recognise these perspectives and work together with the young person by treating them as full partners in promoting their own health. This in turn involves substantial 'direct work' skills – knowing how to relate to children and young people according to their age, ethnicity, culture and ability, in an appropriate manner. Health concerns are fundamentally personal and individual – particularly in areas such as emotional and sexual health – so these direct work skills are essential.

Assessing health needs

One of the challenges of working with children and young people in care in terms of health relates to ensuring that accurate and reliable assessment is undertaken. Of course, each situation will be unique, but there will often be challenges in gathering information from birth families, particularly where there may be a chaotic or abusive birth family background. It may well be the case that in chaotic and disorganised households, children and young people have missed many of their basic health care needs, including for example, regular health checks, inoculations and basic dental care. If this is the case then the initial health intervention with these children and young people may be remedial, that is, it will address disadvantages already experienced prior to the care experience. This is why effective assessment is important and is strongly emphasised in the Guidance issued under the Children Act 1989:

- an assessment of the child's state of health including his/her physical, emotional and mental health;
- the child's health history including, as far as practicable, the child's family's health history;
- the effect of health and health history on the child's development;
- existing arrangements for medical and dental care, appropriate to the child's needs, including:
  - routine checks of the child's general state of health, including dental health
  - treatment and monitoring for identified health or dental care needs
  - preventive measures such as inoculation
  - screening for defects in vision or hearing
  - advice and guidance on promoting health and effective personal care.
  - and planned changes to current arrangements. (DCSF, 2010, p. 24)

But of course it is important to note that assessment itself is not enough as it must be followed through by rigorous professional action. As is the case in many aspects of work with children in care, frequent change of placement can create particular challenges in ensuring that appropriate information follows the child or young person – particularly if that change takes place in an emergency. One of the regular concerns expressed by residential and foster carers is that they are unaware of basic health requirements of the young people they look after, particularly when they are initially placed (Pemberton, 2012). One study of this issue found that some foster carers had actually been dealing with the implications of health challenges for over a year, before they were formally identified (McCarthy, Janeway and Geddes, 2003).

Multi-professional practice

As we seen throughout this book one of the essential aspects of working with children in care is that all professions must work together if the welfare of children in care is to be effectively promoted. Multi-professional practice needs to be underpinned by a number of principles which are outlined in the 'Statutory Guidance on promoting the health and wellbeing of Looked After Children' (2009). This Guidance obliges organisations to:

- Deliver services that are tailored to the individual and diverse needs of children and young people;
- Put the voices of children, young people and their families at the heart of service design and delivery;
- Address health inequalities and emphasise prevention;
- Make sure health needs are accurately assessed and met;
- Deliver excellent, world-class, standards of care;
- Make sure all professionals working with children and young people in care have a clear understanding of the roles and responsibilities of all relevant agencies;
- Be holistic, including considering physical health, sexual, emotional and mental health, wellbeing and health promotion;
- Use integrated working and joint commissioning based around effective partnerships at both strategic and individual case level to improve service delivery, information-sharing, confidentiality and consent. (2009, p. 6)

Here we see that frontline professionals need support and leadership from the organisations they work with if they are to deliver effective health outcomes for young people in care.

The publication 'Healthy Lives, Brighter Futures: the strategy for children and young people's health' (2009) outlines the role of inter-agency co-operation arrangements in enabling health and care authorities to make a reality of partnership to deliver improved health outcomes for children and young people in care.

The social worker has a central role in relation to this process, as the Guidance makes clear:

The child's social worker is responsible for making sure: he or she has a health plan which is drawn up in partnership with the child, his or her carer and (where appropriate) parents, and other agencies and that (while many actions in the plan may be the responsibility of other agencies) the plan is implemented and reviewed in accordance with the regulations. (2009, p. 3)

But the social worker is not, and should not be expected to be, an expert in the delivery of health care or in health assessment: which is why working together with a wide-range of health professionals is crucial. The Guidance suggests that there should be a lead health professional for children in care who will:

- ... ensure the health assessments are undertaken (working with the designated health professionals for looked after children, depending on local arrangements);
- work with the child's social worker to co-ordinate the health care plan and ensure actions are tracked;
- act as a key conduit and contact point between the child or young person and their carer, where they have difficulties accessing health services;
- act as a key health contact for the child's social worker;
- work with the designated health professionals. (2009, p. 43)

Evaluation of dedicated health care teams has demonstrated that these teams achieve positive outcomes and are appreciated by the children and young people themselves (Ryden, 2008).

Providing stability in quality placements

Again we will see that ensuring stability of placement is associated with improvements in outcomes (Stein, 2009, p. 133). Changes of placement may lead to discontinuity of care, loss of information, a decrease in self-esteem and loss of social networks – all of which could contribute to health challenges for children and young people and reduce their resilience. Additionally, changes in school may mean that children and young people miss out on health initiatives and health education that are based in school. It follows that stability of placement is associated with promoting the health care of young people.

Carers will be better able to provide stability if they are aware of the health needs of the young people they look after.

Taking appropriate action following effective assessment

Being in care should enable children to access health services that they may previously have struggled to utilise – indeed research suggests that the health of children and young people in care improves as their placement becomes more secure (Meltzer *et al.* 2003). Promoting the health of those children requires professionals to be pro-active. Having assessed health needs, gathered information and working together with other professionals – it rests with the social worker to ensure that appropriate action takes place and to check that appointments are followed through and that health care is delivered. This process will be overseen at reviews by Independent Reviewing Officers. The review process should be used to ensure that actions are actually delivered.

Addressing lifestyle issues and behavioural challenges, particularly for teenagers in care, provides a major challenge for social workers and direct carers alike. The extensive study carried out by Metzler *et al.* suggests that issues such as smoking, substance abuse and use of alcohol is both higher and starts earlier with young people in care. Of course some of these behaviours may already be undertaken by young people before entering care. Griesbach and Currie (2001) found that whilst this was the case the use of drugs often increased in the care environment – young people stated that this helped them to relax, to forget 'bad things' or to boost their self-confidence.

Providing specific services for care leavers can contribute to ensuring the health of young people once they have left care. For example, one local authority is reported as having developed a range of services for young people encompassing:

- a weekly health drop in run by a leaving care nurse
- A parenting group, providing skills and support sessions for young parents
- a 'cook and eat' group including a café run in association with the youth service
- a weekly football group to promote exercise
- a transition group for 15-year-olds to assist young people in planning for the transition to adulthood.

It is crucially important that sexual health needs are fully addressed as part of a holistic approach to health. The sexual health needs of young people in care are to some extent the same as those in the population at large – including sex education, contraception and advice on safe sex. Some young people in care may have additional needs as they may have been sexually abused or even systematically sexually exploited before or during their time in care. These young people will have additional needs which should be addressed through specialist care and therapeutic services if required.

We can see that health needs are central to an overall approach to promoting the best interests of children and young people in care. We now move on to examine the equally important area of education.

Educational needs of children and young people in care

In many ways the educational needs of children and young people in care are similar to the health challenges we have explored: the young people may have pre-care disadvantage and it requires clearly planned and well-organised multi-professional work to address these disadvantages and to ensure that educational disadvantage does not accumulate once a young person is in care. Again in a similar manner to health being fundamental to all of our life chances, so is education – if a young person leaves care with educational disadvantages they are likely to experience poor outcomes in relation to employment, income, housing and so on.

Educational challenges for children and young people in care

Dependent on their specific individual biography a young person in the care system may well have suffered educational advantage before entering the system. They may have been abused or neglected in the early stages of their life and as a result may suffer from consequent developmental delay (Glaser, 2000; Stone, 2006). Others could have experienced disruption to their early lives through a range of factors – perhaps including domestic violence or substance abuse involving those who cared for them. The British Social Exclusion Unit (2003) calculated that children in care were nine times more likely to have special educational needs when compared with the remainder of the population. Stein links the educational disadvantage of children in care to wider social factors:

> … given accumulated evidence on education and inequality, it follows that the disadvantaged social class position from which young people enter care will have a major influence upon their low educational achievement (Stein, 2001, p. 123)

It is important to note, therefore, that children in care often start with significant disadvantage and in that sense the role of the care system may be to 'add value' (to those outcomes); and that in any case it may be unrealistic to expect 'exit' outcomes to be the same as those in the general ('normative') population.

Once in care, and again echoing the health experiences we have already explored, change of placement may be linked to educational disadvantage. Entering care will often generate a change of school, and if this initial placement was designed to be temporary (as a short-term foster care placement, e.g.), or cannot be sustained for other reasons, this could mean even more changes of school. Many care experienced young people speak of attending many educational settings alongside changes of care placement and social worker. This process can clearly contribute to educational disadvantage: with change of peer networks; change of teachers and teaching styles; a differing emphasis on the curriculum and so on. Thus stability of placement is closely linked to stability of education and to the chance of improved educational outcomes (Jackson, 2001).

Young people in care can also experience disadvantage rooted in the care system: this is sometimes known as system abuse (Frost, Mills and Stein, 1999). An example of this is the experience of stigma – which has a long history in the care system, dating back to the Elizabethan Poor Law (see Frost, Mills and Stein, 1999). Again many care experienced young people will speak of their direct experiences of stigma – being withdrawn from class to attend a review, having the 'wrong' clothes, having to get 'permission' to stay at a friend's house overnight and so on. Whilst many steps have been taken in recent years to address these elements of stigma many potentially stigmatising policies and practices still remain. In England recently the children's rights organisation, A National Voice, have found it necessary to run an imaginative campaign against the phenomenon of young people in care having to pack 'bin bags' when changing placement (anationalvoice. org/blog/updates/2010-the-year-england-goes-bin-bag-free).

Thus we can see the three drivers of educational disadvantage for young people in care: pre-care disadvantage, placement instability and system abuse. These issues can be addressed using of many of the approaches we found useful in addressing health disadvantage – effective planning, partnership working with young people, multi-professional working and targeted approaches to improving educational outcomes. Each of these will be examined in turn.

Effective planning

Essential care planning is essential to address the initial education disadvantage which may face children and young people entering the care system and to ensure that this disadvantage does not accumulate whilst they are in care.

Young peoples' views on their educational experience is mixed:

> It is sad that *over one-in-three care leavers (35 per cent) felt they did not do as well in their education as they might have done if they hadn't come into care.* This is an interesting finding because it is not just a simple statement on the abilities of children in care, but questions whether, given enough stability and encouragement in their lives, more could have achieved what they are capable of. *However, between a quarter and a third of the care leavers (29 per cent) told us they thought they had done better in their education as a result of coming into care. Just over a quarter (27 per cent) thought that coming into care had made no difference to how they had done in their education.* (Ofsted, 2012, p. 36)

It is important that children and young people have clear plans (known in England as Personal Education Plans) that ensure their educational needs are met and regularly reviewed. Of course this will operate more effectively where all parties – including the young person, their carers, social worker and educational staff – are fully involved in this process. Planning needs to positively promote educational opportunities and effectively address any barriers to the young person successfully engaging in education. Barriers can be identified as 'hard' or 'practical' barriers, and might include issues such as financial issues and transport. 'Soft' or 'attitudinal' barriers might include issues such as lack of self-confidence or negative attitudes to education. All barriers demand systematically addressed and planned multi-professional planning.

Working with young people: the concept of resilience

As we keep seeing, children and young people in care should be treated as full partners in all aspects of their lives, wherever possible, if support is to be effective. In terms of education this means assessing what the wishes and needs of the young person are and attempting to make sure that education delivers for them.

Many authors, notably Gilligan (2008), have utilised the concept of 'resilience' to highlight how some young people can succeed in fields such as education, despite disadvantages they initially face. This draws on the earlier work of Rutter, a pioneer in developing the concept of resilience in work with disadvantaged children (Rutter, 1985).

Children and young people can be protected by factors that promote success:

> three broad factors have been associated with resilience: individual characteristics (including temperament, competence, self-efficacy and self-esteem), family support and a supportive person or agency outside of the family (Atwool, 2006, p. 316)

Kendrick (2008) also identifies resilience as a useful concept – he particularly stresses the importance of informal support for young people and argues that this can be under-emphasised in formal service delivery.

Brom *et al.* (2009) argue that resilience is a multi-faceted issue, as it is not:

> ...a universal construct that applies to all life domains. Children may be resilient to specific risk conditions, but quite vulnerable to others. Resilience is a multidimensional phenomenon that is context specific and involves developmental changes. (2008, p. 186)

Contemporary resilience research focuses on applying resilience theory to practice, through appropriate and 'evidence-based' interventions (Daniel and Wassell, 2005), which are essential if resilience is to be a useful construct in supporting young people's education and achievement.

Atwool's work in New Zealand (2006) explored links between resilience and young people in care, and suggested that the vulnerability of children increases as the number of care placements increase, a point supported by research around stability and positive outcomes for young people (Stein, 2010). Change of placement may increase vulnerability, and thus resilience may diminish (with a consequent negative impact on academic achievement). Atwool also found that vulnerability increased where there were ethnic and cultural differences between the child and their current carers. This illustrates close links between placement stability, placement choice, educational achievement and resilience.

A specific study of resilience and young people in the care system was undertaken by McMurray and colleagues (2008) who studied the resilience of young people as they entered the care system. The research team undertook 32 interviews with social workers working with young people in care. They also circulated questionnaires – including, for example, the Rosenberg Self-esteem Scale. The results suggested that social workers struggled to conceptualise resilience and demonstrated a lack of underpinning theory and understanding. Professionals were thus dependent on their own individual understanding of resilience. In some cases the young people sampled by the study were portrayed by social workers as being resilient, which often contradicted the child's actual behaviour and educational progress. McMurray *et al.* suggest that social workers' grasp of the conceptual and research base around resilience is poor and thus they tend to over-emphasise optimistic factors when working with young people in care.

Multi-professional working and targeted approaches

One of the most positive changes in recent years has been the development of multi-professional working with children and young people in the care system (Anning *et al.*, 2010). Whereas, arguably, before the Children Act 1989 children in care would have been seen as a 'problem' belonging to 'the social services', in the current environment, certainly in the United Kingdom, we are moving towards genuinely multi-professional approaches. Young people in care may well have a team of people working with them in their education – which may include social worker, teacher, psychologists and mentors, for example.

In order to address perceived educational disadvantage there are also a number of targeted initiatives in England that work with young people in care. We will explore some of these: the 'virtual head teacher', the 'designated teacher' and the 'personal education plan'.

The virtual head teacher concept was initially piloted as part of the 'Care Matters' programme and then legislated for by the Children and Young Persons Act of 2008. The role was to act as an advocate, champion and co-ordinator for the education of children in care in a given local authority area:

> The virtual school head has introduced a precise and rigorous system for monitoring the progress of looked after children closely, ensuring personalised support is available when required, and holding schools to account for their outcomes (Department for Children, Schools and Families, 2009, p. 31).

The position aims to advocate and promote the school achievements of children and young people in care in their local authority. The virtual head teacher is also accountable for children in care who may be placed 'out of area' and must therefore liaise with colleagues in other areas.

Specifically the virtual head teacher should ensure that schools are aware of children in care, ensure that appropriate added support is provided, and to assist in various ways in promoting the educational performance of young people in care. Further they should promote continuity of schooling and facilitate practical support by ensuring finance is in place things like transport to and from school placement (DCSF, 2009).

Traditionally children in care have been more likely than their peers to be excluded from school and again one role of the virtual head teacher is to reduce this imbalance. In their 1998 study Berridge and Brodie noted that exclusion of children resident in children's homes was seen as inevitable and little seemed to have been done to address this. Certainly the role of the virtual head teacher seems to have raised the profile of this issue to ensure a more pro-active stance is taken (Berridge, 2011).

The 'virtual' role aims to generate resilience among the care population and through this to promote attendance and achievement. The virtual head teacher may also innovate through the use of specific initiatives such personal education allowances, networking, mentoring and communication technology-based initiatives. The local authority (and therefore indirectly the role of the virtual head teacher), is rigorously inspected by Ofsted as part of the inspection regime.

In one of the few studies of the virtual head teacher role, Mayer highlights the qualities required to make this role effective, arguing that the:

> ... successful [virtual head teacher] is ... good at creating vision and setting directions, can define teachers' roles and responsibilities, develop teachers and pupils alike and ultimately manage good teaching and learning. This is all done within a school environment with effective communication, culture and above all trust... (Mayer, 2010, p. 80)

Berridge's evaluation of the pilot found that areas with virtual head teachers were out-performing other authorities in terms of the education of children in care.

Government policy has also suggested that a designated teacher should be appointed in each school, to act in a liaison role to improve the educational achievement of children and young people in care.

The designated teacher's role complements that of the virtual head teacher and includes the requirement to implement and co-ordinate personal education plans, act as an advocate, and to play the role of the educational contact for all relevant professionals (Cocker and Allain, 2010). Mayer supports this role and argues that the designated teacher acts 'as a point of reference for all agencies concerned … effectively wrapp[ing] a bespoke team around the (child)' (2010, p. 43).

Designated teachers can also act as 'champion[s] for children and young people in care in the school setting and encourage good practice and high expectations of children in care' (Holland & Randerson, 2006, p. 95). They also have a key role in challenging the high rate of exclusions of children in care (Fletcher-Campbell *et al.*, 2003).

The personal education plan (PEP) is a tool that aims to maximise the academic achievement of children in care by ensuring access to services and support, setting and monitoring goals, recording progress and achievements, and promoting the stability of the school setting (Holland & Randerson, 2006).

It is essential that PEPs include the views and wishes of young people regarding their needs and support provision (Fletcher-Campbell *et al.*, 2003). PEPs effectively utilised can promote planning, increase the focus on educational needs and should act to reinforce corporate parenting through effective inter-agency working (Fletcher-Campbell *et al.*, 2003). They can also help, early in the process, to identify any support needed to address under-achievement and thereby help promote educational attainment (Fletcher-Campbell *et al.*, 2003, Department for Education and Skills, 2006).

The initiatives outlined above have certainly enhanced inter-professional working, as they rely on collaboration between social workers and teachers to complete and monitor the educational achievement of children in care (Harker *et al.*, 2004).

Care leavers, as a consequence of education under-achievement, are over-represented among young people who are not in Education, Employment or Training (NEET) – in 2010, 38 per cent of care leavers were so classified (DfE, 2010).

Children who have left care are under-represented in further and higher education. Again PEPs as a tool can promote educational attainment for young people in care, and afford young people the opportunity to consider and investigate higher education in an informed manner (Department for Education and Skills, 2006). Jackson *et al.* (2003) state that:

> If we could make coming into care a path to educational success as it is in some other countries, we would not only transform the lives of the children concerned but save immense amounts of public money. The cost of our past failure to educate children in care can be counted in billions' (Jackson *et al.*, 2003, p. 102).

The SEU (2003) also highlights initiatives in relation to further and higher education, where government regulation and specific projects, such as a now discontinued initiative known as 'Aim Higher', has promoted higher educational opportunities for young people in care and leaving care. Sonia Jackson and colleagues have undertaken considerable research in this field and point out that in the period from 2003 until 2010 the number of care leavers going to university has increased from 1 in 100 to around 10 in 100. The Jackson study of care leavers attending university explored issues around money, accommodation, coursework, the law, support and drop-out, and made concrete recommendations for improving the recruitment of young care leavers to university and their retention once they are there (Institute of Education, 2011).

Conclusion

In this chapter we have explored how good practice in the care system can promote positive health and educational outcomes for children and young people. Central themes including working with the young person, effective planning and co-ordinated multi-disciplinary work have emerged as essential for improving the quality and outcomes of the care experience.

9 What future for children and young people in care?

> I am working with young people in care now. We go to foster homes, residential homes and see how we can make it better. If you had asked me when I left care would you like to work with young people in care I would have gone 'you're having a laugh aren't you!' But now I am doing it.
>
> (Jennifer, in care late 1990s and 2000s)

In this conclusion we are more speculative than in preceding chapters, drawing on the research and arguments made throughout this book to suggest what the future of the care system might look like.

A robust system of social justice

Underpinning all discussions about children in care should be a focus on the wider questions of social justice and equality. Many of the more technical texts about the care system – which often have a focus on 'damaged children and young people' – tend to miss this fundamental issue about the care system. Children in care are, almost exclusively, children of the poor and marginalised. As Wilkinson and Pickett (2009) have persuasively demonstrated, inequality generates poor outcomes across a range of social indicators, and this is true of the care system as well. In fact the care system is in many ways a measure of social policy and attitudes towards children. Where children are undervalued and marginalised this is reflected in the nature of the care system – as we saw with the Rumanian orphanages under Communism. Where a child is valued and invested in we tend to find caring and successful care systems – as in many Northern European countries.

Targeted family support

Even where a successful system of social justice is in place we still need a targeted and specialist system of family support. Universal services are necessary but not sufficient. We have seen throughout this book the qualities required of such services – they are well-organised and well-led services, delivered in partnership with families by high-quality, well-supported professionals. A wide range of targeted family support services are required, particularly on the edge of care to ensure that children and young people only enter the care system when it is it their best interests.

A fluid, flexible and responsive care system

Once again even where we have in place a system of social justice and of targeted family support these systems need to be backed up by a well-led, well-resourced, fluid and flexible care system. What would this look like? First, such a system would be dependent on high-quality professionals and carers. They require social recognition, good quality pay and conditions, and professional training and support. Second, such a system requires fluid boundaries. A system of short-term respite care and extensive supported kinship care would break down the strong dichotomy between being 'in the family' and 'being in care'. When there is a strong barrier between the two it makes the journey across the system too complex and difficult.

A child- and young person-centred system

Perhaps the central challenge facing the care system is to become truly 'child-centred' and to make a reality of the legal concept of the 'paramountcy of the child's welfare'. A child-centred system would actually address all the other issues discussed in this concluding chapter. A child-centred system would be rooted in full participation of young people. This should occur at three levels: individual; group; and collective. At individual level this involves being listened to, fully consulted and involved in the planning process as we have outlined in our chapter on leaving care. At group level, since young people live in a group in foster care or residential care, they should participate fully in decision-making on everyday living issues (such as decor and diet) and on policy issues. Young people also need to participate fully at a collective level. This can take a number of forms and perhaps has been one of the most progressive developments of the last two or three decades. Young people have helped in organisations, come together often with support from adults in organisations such as NAYPIC (National Association of Young People in Care) and ANV (A National Voice); see Stein, 2011, for an excellent account of these developments. In England, as part of the 'Care Matters' initiative, local authorities have formed Children in Care Councils which campaign on issues that have an impact on young people in care. These and many other initiatives illustrate how young people can be active in constructing their own futures, and why they should not be seen as passive victims of poor parenting.

Investing in carers and professionals

As the Ofsted report quoted earlier pointed out, 'it was the quality of the professional involved, significantly the key professional, which was the crucial factor in helping to achieve success' (Ofsted, 2011a, p. 4). Sinclair and colleagues found that leadership was central in establishing the 'good' children's home and that in the context of foster care, 'carer characteristics' have been found to be predictive of the success or failure of placements (Sinclair, 2010). Glisson and Hemelgarn (1998) argued that it was the role of the professional that made a key difference for young people, rather than elaborate procedures and organisational structures. These and many other findings suggest that it is the quality of human interaction that makes the key difference for young people and therefore that is a central aspect of improving the care system. An effective care system therefore would invest significantly in supporting carers and professionals – including social workers, foster carers and residential staff. As Berridge *et al.* argue:

> A body of child welfare research in England has concluded that, while working methods are important, quality of care and outcomes for children are more likely to be related to leadership and staffing quality rather than organisational features (Berridge *et al.*, 2011, p. 254)

A positive view of children and young people in care

It has been highlighted throughout this book how research has identified that 'those involved in corporate parenting have lower aspirations for, and expectations of, young people in public care, both in terms of achievement and behaviour' (Taylor, 2005, p. 45) This would seem to be confirmed by the routine police presence in some children's residential settings. Such attitudes fail to appreciate the extraordinary achievements of many children and young people in care in the face of adversity, and such attitudes may become a self-fulfilling prophecy. Raising expectations among professionals of what the care population can and should achieve is surely the way to begin moving towards the realisation of promoting the best interests of each individual young person.

We hope that this book has made a small contribution towards a positive future for children and young people in care.

Bibliography

Acheson, D. (1998) *Independent Inquiry into Inequalities in Health*, London, TSO.

Action on Aftercare (2004) *Setting the Agenda: what's left to do in leaving care?* London: NCH.

Action for Children (2011) Aftercare, London: Action for Children.

Adolescent and Children's Trust (2008) *Care Experience and Criminalisation: An Executive Summary.*

Allen, B.S. & Varca, J.S. (2011) Bring Back Orphanages – an alternative to foster care, *Children and Youth Services Review*, 33, 1067–71.

Allen, G. (2011) Early Intervention: the next steps, London: Cabinet Office.

Anning, A., Cottrell, D., Frost, N., Green, J. and Robinson, M. (2010), *Developing Multi-professional Teamwork for Integrated Children's Services*, Open University Press, Maidenhead.

Atwool, N. (2006), Attachment and Resilience: Implications for Children in Care, *Child Care in Practice*, 12:4, 315–30.

BAAF (2012) Statistics: Northern Ireland, http://www.baaf.org.uk

Barter, C. (2008) Prioritising Young People's Concerns in Residential Care: Responding to Peer Violence. In Kendrick, A. (ed.), *Residential Child Care: Prospects and Challenges*, London: Jessica Kingsley.

Barter, C., Renold. E., Berridge, D. & Cawson, P. (2004) *Peer Violence in Children's Residential Care,* Basingstoke: Palgrave.

Bean, P. & Melville, J. (1990) *Lost Children of the Empire,* London: Unwin Hyman.

Bebbington, A. & Miles, J. (1989) The Background of Children who Enter Care, *British Journal of Social Work*, 19:5, 349–68.

Biehal, N., Dixon, J., Parry, E., Sinclair, I., Green, J., Roberts, C., Kay, C., Rothwell, J., Kapadia, D. & Roby, A. (2012) *(CaPE) Evaluation of Multidimensional Treatment Foster Care for Adolescents (MTFC-A)*, London, Department for Education-Research Brief 194.

Bellfield, C.R., Noves, M. & Barrett, W.S. (2006) *High/Scope Perry Pre-School Program: Cost Benefit Analysis using data from the age 40 year follow up*, NIEER: New Brunswick, NJ.

Belsky, J., Barnes, J. & Melhuish, E. (2007) *The National Evaluation of Sure Start*, Bristol: Policy.

Berridge, D. (2010) Reflections on Child Welfare Research and the Policy Process: the Virtual School Head and the Education of Looked-After Children, *British Journal of Social Work,* 42, 26–41.

Berridge, D. & Brodie, I. (1998) *Children's Homes Revisited,* London: Jessica Kingsley.

Berridge, D., Biehal, N., Lutman, E., Henry, L. & Palomares, M. (2011) *Raising the Bar? Evaluation of the social pedagogy pilot programme,* London: Department for Education.

Berrington, A., Stone, J., & Falkingham, J. (2009) The Changing living arrangements of young adults in the UK, *Population Trends,* London: TSO.

Biehal, N., Ellison. S. & Sinclair, I. (2011) Intensive fostering: an independent evaluation of MTFC in an English setting, *Children and Youth Services Review,* 33, 2043–9.

Blair, T. (1998) *The Third Way: New politics for the new century,* Fabian Pamphlet 588, London: Fabian Society.

Blair, T. (2000) Foreword to *Adoption – a Performance and Innovation Unit Report,* London: Department of Health.

Boswell, J. (1988) *The Kindness of Strangers: the abandonment of children in Western Europe from Late Antiquity to the Renaissance,* Harmondsworth: Penguin.

Bowlby, J. (1953) *Child Care and the Growth of Love,* Harmondsworth: Pelican.

British Association for Adoption and Fostering (2012) Statistics: Northern Ireland, www.baaf.org.uk

Brodie, I. and Morris, M. (2009) *Improving Educational Outcomes for Looked-after Children and Young People,* London: C4EO.

Brom, D., Pat-Horenczyk, R. & Ford, J. (2009) Treating Traumatised Children: Risk, Resilience and Recovery. Hove: Routledge.

Bronfenbrenner, U. (1974) *Two Worlds of Childhood,* Harmondsworth: Penguin.

The British Social Exclusion Unit (2003) – see SEU

Cameron, C., Bennert. K., Simon, A. & Wigfall, V. (2007) *Using Health, Education, Housing and Other Services: A study of care leavers and young people in difficulty,* London: Thomas Coram Research Unit.

Campling, P. and Hague, R. (1999) Therapeutic Communities: Past, present and future. London, Jessica Kingsley, cited in Stevens, I. and Furnival, J. (2008) Therapeutic Approaches in Residential Care. In: Kendrick, A. (ed). *Residential Child Care: Prospects and Challenges.* London, Jessica Kingsley, 196–209.

Carter, I. (2007) *It's Never Too Early… It's Never Too Late - The ACPO Strategy for Children and Young People,* London: ACPO.

Centre for Excellence and Outcomes, Community Care (2010a), 7 January 2010, 24–5.

Centre for Excellence and Outcomes (2010b) *Early Intervention – Early messages from effective local practice 'call for evidence',* London: Centre for Excellence in Outcomes for Children.

Centre for Excellence and Outcomes (2011) *Grasping the Nettles,* London: Centre for Excellence in Outcomes for Children.

Chipenda-Dansokho, S, Little, M. & Thomas, B. (2003) *Residential Services for Children: Definitions, numbers and classifications,* Chicago: Chaplin Hall Centre for Children, University of Chicago.

Clough, R. (2000) *The Practice of Residential Work*, Basingstoke: Macmillan.

Clough, R, Bullock, R. & Ward, A. (2006) *What Works in Residential Child Care: A review of the research evidence and the practical considerations*, London: National Children's Bureau.

Cocker C. & Allain, L. 2010, *Social Work with looked-after children,* Exeter, Learning Matters.

Colton, M. & Roberts, S. (2007) Factors that contribute to high turnover among residential child care staff, *Child and Family Social Work*, 12(2), 133–52.

Colwell (1974) *Report of the Committee of Inquiry into the Care and Supervision provided by local authorities and other agencies in Relation to Maria Colwell and the co-ordination between them* (Chairman: T.G. Field-Fisher) London, Her Majesty's Stationery Office.

Cunha, F. & Heckman, J. (2006) *Investing in our Young People*, Chicago: University of Chicago.

Daniel, B. (2008) The Concept of Resilience: Messages for Residential Child Care. In: Kendrick, A. (ed). *Residential Child Care: Prospects and challenges*, London: Jessica Kingsley.

Daniel, B. & Wassell, S. (2002a) *Adolescence: Assessing & Promoting Resilience in Vulnerable Children III,* London: Jessica Kingsley.

Daniel, B. & Wassell, S. (2002b) *The School Years: Assessing & Promoting Resilience in Vulnerable Children II,* London: Jessica Kingsley.

Daniel, B. & Wassell, S. (2005) *Resilience: A Framework for Positive Practice.* Edinburgh: Scottish Executive. www.scotland.gov.uk/Resource/Doc/920/0011997. pdf, accessed 30 April 2007.

Davies, C. & Ward, H. (2012) *Safeguarding Children Across Services: Messages from research*, London, Jessica Kingsley Press.

Davies, M. (2012) Social Work with Children and Families, London, Palgrave

Davis, L. (2010) *A Practical Guide to Fostering Law-Fostering Regulations, Child Care Law and the Youth Justice System,* London: Jessica Kingsley.

Deloitte MCS Ltd (2007) *Determining the Optimum Supply of Children's Residential Care*, London: DCSF.

Department for Children, Schools and Families (2010) *The Children Act 1989 Guidance and Regulations Volume 2: Care planning, placement and case review*, London, DCSF.

Department for Children, Schools & Families (2007) *Time for Change,* London: Stationery Office.

Department for Children, Schools & Families (2008) *Care Matters: Time to deliver for children in care,* London: DCSF.

Department for Children, Schools & Families (2009) *The Virtual Headteacher: Guidance*, London, DCSF.

Department for Children, Schools & Families. (2010a) *The Children Act 1989 Guidance & Regulation: Volume 2: care placement, planning & case review*, London: DCSF.

Department for Children, Schools & Families. (2010b) *Independent Reviewing Officer Handbook: Statutory Guidance for IROs & local authorities on their functions in relation to case management & reviews for looked after children*, London: DCSF.

Department for Education (2010) *Family and Friends Care: Statutory Guidance for Local Authorities*, London, DfE.

Department for Education (2010) *Children Looked After by Local Authorities in England (including adoption & care leavers), Year Ending 31 March 2010.* Statistical First Release: 30 September 2010, London: DfE.

Department for Education (2010) *The Children Act 1989 Guidance and Regulation: Volume 3: Planning the transition to adulthood for care leavers,* London: DCSF.

Department for Education (2011) *The Foster Carer's Charter,* London, DfE.

Department for Education (2011a) *Foster Carer's Charter,* DfE. www.education. gov.uk/childrenandyoungpeople/families/childrenincare/fostercare/a0071236/ charter-for-foster-care

Department for Education (2011b) Children Act 1989 Guidance and Regulations Volume 4: Fostering Services, http://publications.education.gov.uk/ref: DfE-00023-2011.

Department for Education (2011c), *An Action Plan for Adoption: Tackling delay,* London: DfE.

Department for Education (2012): *Children Looked After by Local Authorities in England (including adoption and care leavers) – year ending 31 March 2012,* Statistical First Release, 25 September 2012.

Department for Education and Skills (2003) *Every Child Matters.* London: DfES.

Department for Education and Skills (2004) *Every Child Matters: Change for Children.* London: DfES.

Department for Education and Skills (2006) *Care Matters: Transforming the lives of children and young people in care,* London: DfES.

Department for Education and Skills (2007) *Care Matters: Time for change.* London: DfES.

Department of Health (1998) *The Quality Protects Programme: Transforming children's services.*

Department of Health (2002) *Promoting the Health of Looked After Children,* London, Department of Health

Department of Health (2009) *Healthy Lives, Brighter Futures: the strategy for children and young people's health,* London: Department of Health.

Department of Health/Department for Children, Schools and Families (2009) *Statutory Guidance on promoting the health and wellbeing of Looked After Children,* London, DCSF.

Driver, S. & Martell, L. (1997) New Labour's Communitarianisms. In *Critical Social Policy,* 17(3): 27–46.

Duncalf, Z. (2010) *Listen Up! Adult Care Leavers Speak Out: The views of 310 care leavers aged 17–78.* Manchester: Care Leavers' Association.

Emond, R. (2003) Putting the Care into Residential Care: The Role of Young People, *Journal of Social Work,* Vol 3(3), 321–37.

Emond, R. (2008) Children's Voices, Children's Rights. In: Kendrick, A. (ed). *Residential Child Care: Prospects and challenges,* London: Jessica Kingsley.

Etzioni, A. (1993) *The Spirit of Community: Rights, responsibilities and the communitarian agenda,* New York: Simon and Schuster.

Evan B Donaldson Institute (2008) Finding Families for African American Children, New York, Evan B Donaldson Institute.

Farmer, E. & Pollock, S. (1998) *Sexually Abused & Abusing Children in Substitute Care*, Chichester: Wiley.

Farmer, E., Moyers, S. & Lipscombe, J. (2004) *Fostering Adolescents*, London: Jessica Kingsley.

Fawcett, B, Featherstone, B. & Goddard, J. (2004) *Contemporary child care policy & practice*, Basingstoke: Palgrave Macmillan.

Featherstone, B. & Dolan, P. (2010) *Family Support Highlight, 225,* London, NCB.

Fildes, V. (1988) *Wet Nursing,* Oxford: Blackwell.

Fitzpatrick, C. (2009) Looked After Children and the Criminal Justice System. In Broadhurst, K., Grover, C and Jamieson, J (eds) *Critical Perspectives on Safeguarding Children*, Chichester, Wiley, pp. 211–225.

Fletcher-Campbell, F., Aracher, T. & Tomlinson, K. (2003) *The Role of the School in Supporting the Education of Children in Public Care*, London, DCSF

Forrester, D., Goodman, G., Cocker, C., Binnie, C. & Jensch, G. (2007*) Does Care Work? A Focused Literature Review on Welfare Outcomes for Children Who Enter Care*, Welsh Assembly Government.

Forrester, D., Goodman, K., Cocker, C., Binnie, C. and Jensch, G. (2009) What is the impact of public care on children's welfare? A review of the research findings from England and Wales, *Journal of Social Policy*, 38(3), 439–56.

Foucault, M. (1977) *Discipline and Punish: The birth of the prison*, New York: Random House.

Fox-Harding, L. (1991) *Perspectives in Child Care Policy*, London: Longman.

France, A. & Utting, D. (2005) The Paradigm of Risk and Protection-Focussed Prevention and its Impact on Services for Children and Families. In *Children & Society*, 19(2): 77–90.

Frost, N. (1992) Implementing the Children Act 1989 in a Hostile Climate. In Carter, P., Jeffs, T. and Smith, M.K. (eds), *Changing Social Work and Welfare*, Buckingham: Open University Press.

Frost, N. (2003) Understanding Family Support in Frost, N., Jeffery, L., & Lloyd, A. (2003), *The RHP Companion to Family Support*, Lyme Regis: RHP.

Frost, N. (2011) *Re-thinking Children and Families*, London, Continuum.

Frost, N. & Dolan, P. (2012) The Theoretical Foundations of Family Support in Social Work with Children and Families. In Davies, M. (ed) *Social Work with Children and Families,* Basingstoke: Palgrave MacMillan.

Frost, N. & Parton, N. (2009) *Understanding Children's Social Care*, London: Sage.

Frost, N. & Stein, M. (1989) *The Politics of Child Welfare: Inequality, power & change,* London: Harvester Wheatsheaf.

Frost, N., Jeffery, L. & Lloyd, A. (2003), *The RHP Companion to Family Support*, Lyme Regis: RHP.

Frost, N, Mills, S and Stein, M. (1999) *Understanding Residential Child Care*, Aldershot: Ashgate.

Gaber, I. & Aldridge, J. (eds) (1994) *In the Best Interests of the Child: Culture, identity & trans-racial adoption*, London: Free Association Books.

Gallagher, B. (2000) The extent and nature of known cases of institutional child sex abuse. In *British Journal of Social Work*, 30, 795–817.

Giddens, A. (1998) *The Third Way: The Renewal of social democracy*, Cambridge: Polity Press.

Gill, O. & Jackson, B. (1983) *Adoption and Race*, London: Batsford.

Giller, H. & Morris, A. (1981) *Care and Discretion: Social work decisions with delinquents*, London: Burnett Books.

Gillies, V. (2008) Perspectives on Parenting Responsibility: Contextualising values and practices. In *Journal of Law and Society*, 35(1): 95–112.

Gilligan, R. (2000) Family Support: Issues and Prospects. In Canavan, J., Dolan, P. and Pinkerton, J. *Family Support: Direction from diversity*, London: Jessica Kingsley.

Gilligan, R. (2008) Promoting Resilience in Young People in long-term care – the relevance of roles and relationships in the domains of recreation and work. In *Journal of Social Work Practice*, 22:1, 37–50.

Gilroy, P. (1994) Foreword in Gaber, I., and Aldridge, J. (eds) (1994) *In the Best Interests of the Child: Culture, identity and trans-racial adoption*, London: Free Association Books.

Glaser, D. (2000) Child Abuse and Neglect and the Brain: A review, *Journal of Child Psychology and Psychiatry*, 41:1, 97–116.

Glass, N. (2005) Some Mistake Surely? *The Guardian*, 5 January.

Glisson, A. & Hemelgarn, C. (1998) The Effects of Organisational Climate and Interorganizational Coordination on the Quality and Outcomes of Children's Services Systems. In *Child Abuse and Neglect*, 22:5, 410–22.

Goffman, E. (1961) *Asylums: Essays on the Social Situation of Mental Patients and Other Inmates*, New York: Doubleday.

Griesbach and Currie (2001) *Health Behaviours of Scottish Schoolchildren: Report 7: Control of adolescent smoking in Scotland*, Child and Adolescent Health Research Unit, University of Edinburgh.

Hannon, C., Wood, C. & Bazalgette, L. (2010) *In Loco Parentis*, London: Demos.

Happer, H., McCreadie, J. and Aldgate, J. (2006) *Celebrating Success: What Helps Looked After Children Succeed*, Edinburgh Social Work Inspection Agency.

Hardiker, P, Exton, K. & Barker, M. (1991) *Policies and Practice in Preventive Child Care*, Aldershot: Avebury.

Harker, R. (2012) Children in Care in England: Statistics, House of Commons Library, www.parliament.uk/briefing-papers/SN04470.pdf

Harker, R., Dobel-Ober, D., Berridge, D. & Sinclair, R. (2004) *Taking Care of Education: An evaluation of the education of looked after children*, London, National Children's Bureau.

Harris, P. (ed) (2006) *In Search of Belonging*, London: BAAF.

Hayden, C. (2010) Offending Behaviour in Care: Is children's residential care a 'criminogenic' environment? *Child and Family Social Work*, 15, 461–72.

Health Committee, Second Report of the Session 1997–8, *Children Looked After by Local Authorities*, HC 319-I, para 33.

Heckman, J., Moon, S.H., Pinto, R. & Savelyev, P. (2009), The Rate of Return of the High/Scope Perry Pre-School Program, *Discussion Paper 4533*, IZA, Bonn.

Hendrick, H. (2003) *Child Welfare*, Bristol: Policy Press.

Heywood, J. (1965) *Children in Care*, London: Routledge

Hilton, Z. & Mills, C. (2007) 'Ask the Children', *Criminal Justice*, 16:16–18.

Hirschi, T. (1969) *Causes of Delinquency*, Berkley, University of California Press.

Holland, J. & Randerson, C. (2006) Supporting Children in Public Care in Schools, London, JKP.

Holman, B. (1998) *From Children's Departments to Family Departments, Child and Family Social Work*, Vol. 3(3), 205–11.

House of Commons Health Select Committee (1998) *Children Looked After by Local Authorities* (HC 319-1), London, The Stationery Office.

House of Commons (2011) *Looked-after Children: Further Government Response to the Third Report from the Children, Schools and Families Committee, Session 2008-09*, Education Committee, 4 April 2011; www.parliament.co.uk

Howley, D. (2011) Foster carers cannot take the place of parents, *Guardian*, 22 June 2011.

Idaho Coalition of Home Educators, *Preschool's Magic Blackbox: Critique of the Perry High/Scope program*, www.iche-idaho.org/issues/34.

Institute of Education (2011) *Case Study on the Impact of IoE Research into 'Going to University from Care'*, London:IoE.

Jackson, S. (2001) *Nobody Ever Told Us School Mattered: Raising the educational attainments of children in care*, London: British Agencies for Adoption and Fostering.

Jackson, S. (2003) Care past and present. In Chase, E., Simon, A. and Jackson, S. (eds*), In Care and After: A positive perspective*, London: Routledge.

Jones, C. (2001) Voices from the Front Line: State Social Work and New Labour, *British Journal of Social Work*, 31(4): 547–62.

Kendrick, A. (1998) Abuse of children in residential and foster care: A brief review, Scottish Institute for Residential Child Care (SIRCC) www.sircc.strath.ac.uk/research/kendrick.html.

Kendrick, A. (2008) Introduction: Residential Childcare. In: Kendrick, A. (ed). *Residential Child Care: Prospects and challenges*. London: Jessica Kingsley.

Kilpatrick, R., Berridge, D., Sinclair, R., Larkin, E., Lucas, P.J., Kelly, B. & Geraghty, T. (2008) *Working with Challenging and Disruptive Situations in Residential Child Care: Sharing effective practice*, London: Social Care Institute for Excellence.

Kirton, D. (2000) *'Race', Ethnicity and Adoption*, OUP: Buckingham.

Laming Report (2003) *The Victoria Climbié Inquiry: Report of an Inquiry by Lord Laming* (Cm5730), London: The Stationery Office.

Layder, D. (2006) *Understanding Social Theory*, London: Sage.

Layder, D. (2004) *Emotion in Social Life: The lost heart of society*, London, Sage.

Lee, R.M. (2003) The Transracial Adoption Paradox. In *Counselling Psychology*, 31: 6, 711–44.

Lerch, V. & Stein, M. (2010) *Aging Out of Care: From care to adulthood in European and Central Asian societies,* California, SOS Children's Villages.

Little, M. and Kelly, S. (1995) *A Life without Problems? The Achievements of a Therapeutic Community*. Aldershot: Arena. Cited in Stevens, I. and Furnival, J. (2008) Therapeutic Approaches in Residential Care. In: Kendrick, A. (ed). *Residential Child Care: Prospects and Challenges*. London, Jessica Kingsley, 196–209.

Luckock, B. (2008) Adoption Support and the Negotiation of Ambivalence in Family Policy and Children's Services, *Journal of Law and Society,* 35(1): 3–27.

Luckock, B. & Hart, A. (2005) Adoptive family life and adoption support: policy ambivalence and the development of effective services. In *Child and Family Social Work* 10.

Macleod, S., Hart, R., Jeffes, J. and Wilkin, A. (2010) *The Impact of the Baby Peter Case on Applications for Care Orders*, LGA Research Report, Slough, NFER.

Mayer, J. (2010) The impact of the Virtual Head Teacher, Nottingham, unpublished.

McCann, J.B., James, A., Wilson, S. & Dunn, G. (1996) Prevalence of Psychiatric Disorders in Young People in the Care System. In *British Medical Journal* 313, 1529–30.

McCarthy, G., Janeway, J. and Geddes, A. (2003) The impact of emotional and behavioural problems on the lives of children growing up in the care system. In *Adoption and Fostering*, 27(3), 14–19.

McKenzie, R.B. (1999) *Rethinking Orphanages for the 21st Century*, California: Sage.

McLaughlin, K. (2007) Regulation and Risk in Social Work: The General Social Care Council and the Social Care Register in Context, *British Journal of Social Work*, 37 (7), 1263–77.

McMurray, I., Connolly, H., Preston-Shoot, M. & Wigley, V (2008) Constructing Resilience: social workers' understandings and practice, Health and Social Care in the Community, 16:3, 299–309.

Melhuish, E. & Hall, D. (2007) The policy background to Sure Start, in Belsky, J., Barnes, J. and Melhuish, E. (eds) *The National Evaluation of Sure Start – does area-based early intervention work?* Bristol: Policy Press.

Meltzer, H., Corbin, T., Gatward, R., Goodman, R., Ford, T. (2003) *The Mental Health of Young People Looked-after by Local Authorities in England*, London: TSO.

Mitchell, F. (2003) The Social Services response to unaccompanied children in England. In *Child and Family Social Work,* 8(3):179–89.

Morgan, P. (1998) *Adoption and the Care of Children*, London: IEA.

Morgan, R. (2007) One of the truly remarkable changes from Old to New Labour is that incarcerating more young people is viewed as an achievement, *Professional Social Work*, March: 16–17.

Morgan, R. (2009) *Life in Children's Homes: A Report of Children's Experience*, Manchester: Ofsted.

Morgan, R. (2011) *Messages for Munro: A report of children's views collected for Professor Eileen Munro by the Children's Rights Director for England,* Manchester: Ofsted.

Morgan, R. & Newburn, T. (2007) 'Youth Justice.' In Maguire, M., Morgan, R. and Reiner, R. (eds), *The Oxford Handbook of Criminology*, 4th edn, Oxford: Oxford University Press.

Morris, S. & Wheatley, H. (1994) *Time to Listen: The Experience of Young People in Foster and Residential Care*, London: ChildLine.

Mrazek, P.J. & Haggerty, R.J. (eds), (1994) *Reducing Risks for Mental Disorders: Frontiers for Preventive Intervention Research*, Washington DC: Institute of Medicine/National Academy Press.

Muncie, J. (2000) Pragmatic Realism? Searching for Criminology in The New Youth Justice. In Goldson, B. (ed), *The New Youth Justice*, Lyme Regis: Russell House Publishing.

Muncie, J. (2004) *Youth and Crime*, London: Sage.

Munro, E. (2001) Empowering Looked-after Children. In *Child and Family Social Work*, 6, 129–37.

Munro, E. (2004a) The Impact of Audit on Social Work Practice. In *British Journal of Social Work*, 34(8): 1079–95.

Munro, E. (2004b) State Regulation of Parenting. In *Political Quarterly*, 75(2): 180–5.

Munro, E.R., Lushey, C. and Ward, H. (2011) *Evaluation of the RIGHT2Bcared4 pilots: Final Report*, Department for Education: London.

Nacro (2003) *Reducing offending by looked after children: Good practice guide*. London: Nacro.

Nacro (2005) *A Handbook on Reducing Offending by Looked After Children*. London: Nacro.

Narey, M. (2007) *Beyond Care Matters: Future of the Care Population Working Group Report*, London: HM Government.

Narey, M. (2011) *Narey Report on Adoption*, Supplement to *The Times*, 5 July.

National Care Advisory Service *et al.* (2012) *Access All Areas*, London: NCAS.

National Care Association (2009) *Every Budget Matters: A Survey of the Current Commissioning Practices and the Health of the Residential Child Care Sector*. London.

National Children's Bureau (2008) *Healthy Care Briefing*, London: NCB.

National Evaluation of Sure Start (2008) *The Impact of SSLP's on Child Development and Family Functioning*, Birkbeck: NESS.

NICE (2010) *Promoting the quality of life of looked-after children and young people*, London: NICE/SCIE.

Ofsted (2001) *Raising Achievement of Children in Public Care: A Report from the Office of Her Majesty's Chief Inspector of Schools*, Manchester: Ofsted.

Ofsted (2011a) *Edging Away from Care: How services successfully prevent young people entering care*, Manchester: Ofsted.

Ofsted (2011b) *Children on Independent Reviewing Officers: a report of children's views by the Children's Rights Director for England*, Manchester: Ofsted.

Ofsted (2012) *After Care: Young people's views on leaving care*, Manchester: Ofsted.

Olds, D., Henderson, C.R., Cole, R., Eckerode, J., Kitzman, H., Luckey, D., Pettit, L., Sidora, H., Morris, P. & Powers, J. (1998) Long-term Effects of Nurse Home Visitation on Children's Criminal and Antisocial Behaviour. In *Journal of American Medical Association*, 280: 1238–44.

O'Neill, T. (2008) Gender Matters in Residential Child Care. In Kendrick, A. (ed). *Residential Child Care: Prospects and Challenges*, London: Jessica Kingsley.

Ormerod, P. (2005) The Impact of Sure Start. In *Political Quarterly*, 76(4): 565–7.

Page, R. & Clarke, G. (eds) (1977) *Who Cares*, London: National Children's Bureau.

Parker, R., Ward, H., Jackson, S., Aldgate, J. & Wedge, P. (eds), (1991) *Looking After Children: Assessing Outcomes in Child Care. The Report of an Independent Working Party established by the Department of Health*, London: HMSO.

Parker, R. (1988) Children. In Sinclair, I. (ed) *Residential Care: The Research Reviewed*. London, HMSO.

Parker, R. (ed) (1999) *Adoption Now: Messages from Research*, Chichester: Wiley.

Parks, G. (2000) The High/Scope Perry Pre-school Programme. In *Juvenile Justice Bulletin*.

Pemberton, C. (2012) Most Social Workers Cite Problems with Social Workers. In *Community Care*, 18 July.

Penn, H. & Gough, D. (2002) The price of a loaf of bread: some conceptions of family support. *Children & Society* 16:1 17–32.

Petrie, P., Boddy, J., Cameron, C., Wigfall., V and Simon, A. (2006) *Working with Children in Care: European perspectives*, Buckingham: Open University Press.

Pinkerton, J. & Dolan, P. (2007) Family support, social capital, resilience and adolescent coping. In *Child & Family Social Work,* 12, 219–28.

Rowe, J. & Lambert, L. (1973) *Children Who Wait: A study of children needing substitute families*, London: British Association for Adoption and Fostering.

Rubin, D.M., O'Reilly, A.L. Luan, X. and Localio, A.R. (2007) The Impact of Placement Stability on Behavioural Well-being for Children in Foster Care. In *Paediatrics* 119 (2), 336–44.

Rushton, A. & Dance, C. (2006) The Adoption of Children from Public Care: A Prospective Study of Outcome in Adolescence. In *Journal of the American Academy of Child & Adolescent Psychiatry* 45(7) 877–83.

Rushton, A. & Monck, E. (2009) *Enhancing Adoptive Parenting: A randomised controlled Trial of Adoption Support*, DCSF: London.

Rutter, M. (1985) Resilience in the Face of Adversity: Protective factors and resistance to psychiatric disorder. In *British Journal of Psychiatry*, 147, 598–611.

Rutter, M. (2006) Is Sure Start an Effective Preventive Intervention? In *Child and Adolescent Mental Health,* 11(3): 135–41.

Rutter, M. (2007) Sure Start Local Programmes: an outsiders perspective, in Belsky, J., Barnes, J. and Melhuish, E. (eds) *The National Evaluation of Sure Start – does area-based early intervention work?* Bristol: Policy Press.

Ryden, N. (2008) Report of an Evaluation of the Health Care team for looked-after children, Unpublished.

Saunders, L. & Broad, B. (1997) *The Health Needs of Young People Leaving Care*, Leicester, De Montfort University.

Schweinhart, L., Barnes, H. and Weikhart, D. (eds) (1993) *Significant Benefits: the High/Scope Perry Pre-School Study through age 27,* Ypsilanti, High/Scope Press.

SCIE, (2007) The Social Care Needs of Children with Complex Health and Social Care Needs and their Families. In *Knowledge Review 18*, scie.org.uk.

SCIE (2010) *The social care needs of refugees and asylum seekers,* www.scie.org.uk

The Scottish Government (2012) *Children Looked After: High Level Summary of Statistics Trend.* Last update, 29 February 2012, www.scotland.gov.uk

Scourfield, P. (2007) Are there reasons to be worried about the 'cartelisation' of residential care? *Critical Social Policy,* 27:2, 15581.

Scott, J. and Ward, H. (2008) The Health of Looked-After Children in Residential Care. In Kendrick, A (ed) *Residential Child Care: Prospects and challenges*, London, JKP.

Secretary of State for Social Services (1974) *Report of the Inquiry into the Care and Supervision Provided in Relation to Maria Colwell*, London: HMSO.

Sempik, J., Ward, H. and Darker, I. (2008), Emotional and Behavioural Difficulties of Children and Young People at Entry into Care. In *Clinical Child Psychology and Psychiatry*, 13:2, 221-33.

Shaw, J. (2010) *From Residential Care to Custody: Young, Looked-after and Criminalised?* PhD Thesis, Leeds Metropolitan University.

Silverman, A.R. (1993) Outcomes of Transracial Adoption, *The Future of Children*, 3:1, 105–18.

Simmonds, J. (2012) Adoption: from the preservation of the moral order to the needs of the child, in Davies, M. (ed) *Social Work with Children and Families,* Palgrave Macmillan, Basingstoke.

Sinclair, R. (1998) Involving children in Planning Their Care, *Child and Family Social Work*, 3, 137–42.

Sinclair, I. (2005) *Fostering Now: Messages from Research*, London: Jessica Kingsley.

Sinclair, I. (2010) What Makes for Effective Foster Care: Some Issues. In Fernandez, E. and Barth, R. (eds) *How Does Foster Care Work: International Evidence on Outcomes,* London: Jessica Kingsley

Sinclair, I. & Gibbs, I. (1998) *Children's Homes: A Study in Diversity*, Chichester: Wiley.

Sinclair, I., Baker, C., Lee, J. and Gibbs, I. (2007) *The Pursuit of Permanence: A Study of the English Care System,* London: Jessica Kingsley.

Sinclair, I., Gibbs, I. & Wilson, K. (2004) *Foster Carers: Why They Stay & Why They Leave*, London: Jessica Kingsley.

Sinclair, I., Wilson, K. & Gibbs, I. (2005) *Foster Placements: Why They Succeed & Why They Fail*, London: Jessica Kingsley.

Sinclair, I., Baker, C., Wilson, K. & Gibbs, I. (2005) *Foster Children: Where They Go & How They Do,* London: Jessica Kingsley.

Singh, S. (2005) Thinking Beyond 'Diversity': Black and minority ethnic children in Scotland. In Crimmens, D. and Milligan, I. (eds) *Facing Forward: residential child care in the 21st century*, Lyme Regis: RHP.

Skinner, A. (1992) *Another Kind of Home: A review of residential child care*, Edinburgh: The Scottish Office.

Skinner, C. (2003) New Labour and Family Policy. In Bell, M. and Wilson, K. (eds), *The Practitioners' Guide to Working with Families*, Basingstoke: Palgrave Macmillan.

Small, J. (1986) *Transracial Placements*: Conflicts and Contradictions. In S. Ahmed, J. Cheetham, and J. Small, *Social Work with Black Children and Their Families* (eds.) London, Batsford.

Smith, E. (1996) Bring Back the Orphanages? In *A History of Child Welfare,* Smith, E. and Merkel-Holguin, L. (eds), New Brunswick: Transaction.

Smith, M. (2009) *Rethinking Residential Child Care: Positive perspectives*, Bristol: Policy Press.

Smith, R. (2007) *Youth Justice: Ideas, Policy, Practice*, Cullompton: Willan.

Social Exclusion Unit (2003) A Better Education for Children in Care. Cabinet Office, London.

Statham, J. & Smith, M. (2010) *Issues in Earlier Intervention: Identifying and supporting children with additional needs*, London: DCSF.

Stein, M. (2001) Leaving Care, Education and Career Trajectories. In Jackson, S. (2001) *Nobody Ever Told Us School Mattered: Raising the educational attainments of children in care*, London: British Agencies for Adoption and Fostering.

Stein, M. (2004) *What Works for Young People Leaving Care?* Barkingside: Barnardos.

Stein, M. (2006) Wrong turn, *The Guardian*, Wednesday 6 December.

Stein, M. (2009) Quality Matters in Children's Services, London, JKP.

Stein, M. (2011) Care Less Lives, London, NCAS.

Stein, M. & Carey, K. (1986) *Leaving Care,* Oxford: Blackwell.

Stein, M. & Ward, H. (2011) International Perspectives on Young People's Transitions from Care to Adulthood. In *Children & Youth Services Review* 33, 2409–11.

Stevens, I and Furnival, J. (2008) Therapeutic Approaches in Residential Care. In: Kendrick, A. (ed). *Residential Child Care: Prospects and Challenges.* London, Jessica Kingsley, 196–209.

Stewart, J, Smith, D, Stewart, G. & C. Fullwood. (1994) *Understanding Offending Behaviour,* Harlow: Longman.

Stone, S. (2006), Child Maltreatment, Out-of-home Placement and Academic Vulnerability: A fifteen-year review of the evidence and future directions. In *Children and Youth Services Review*, 23:2, 139–61.

Taylor, C. (2005) *Young People in Care and Criminal Behaviour*, London: Jessica Kingsley.

Thoburn, J. (2008) *Children in Public Out of Home Care: 21 years of policy, London,* Action for Children.

Thoburn J. & Courtney, M.E. (2011), A Guide Through the Knowledge Base on Children in Out-Of-Home Care, *Journal of Children's Services* 6:4, 210-27.

Thoburn, J., Norford, L. and Parvez Rashid, S. (2000) *Permanent Family Placement for Children of Minority Ethnic Origin*, London: Jessica Kingsley.

Thomas, N. (2000) *Children, Family and the State: Decision-making and child participation*, Macmillan: Basingstoke.

Thorpe, D., Smith, D., Green, C. & Paley, J. (1980) *Out of Care: The Community Support for Juvenile Offenders*, London: Allen and Unwin.

Tizard, B. & Phoenix, A. (1993) *Black, White or Mixed Race,* London: Routledge.

Tunstill, J. & Allnocks, D. (2007) *Understanding the Contribution of Sure Start Local Programmes to the Task of Safeguarding Children's Welfare. Sure Start Report 026,* The National Evaluation of Sure Start Team, Birkbeck College: London.

Turney, D. & Tanner, K. (2003) What do we Know about Child Neglect? A critical review of the literature and its application to social work practice. In *Child and Family Social Work*, Vol. 8, 25–34.

Ungar, M. (2005) *Pathways to Resilience among Children in Child Welfare, Corrections, Mental Health and Educational Settings*, Navigation and Negotiation Child and Youth Care Forum, 34:6, 423–44.

Ungar, M. (2008) *The Study of Youth Resilience Across Cultures: Lessons from a Pilot Study of Measurement Development,* Research in Human Development, Vol. 5, No. 3, 166–80.

UNICEF (2007) Child Poverty in Perspective: An overview of child well-being in rich countries, *Innocenti Report Card 7*, Florence: UNICEF Innocenti Research Centre.

Utting, W. (1997) *People Like Us: The Report of the Review of the Safeguards for Children Living Away from Home*, London: HMSO.

Utting, W. (1991) *Children in Public Care: A review of residential child care*, London: HMSO.

Van Bienum, M. (2008) Mental Health and Children and Young People in Residential Care. In: Kendrick, A. (ed), *Residential Child Care: Prospects and Challenges*, London: Jessica Kingsley, 47–59.

Wade, J., Biehal, N., Stein, M. and Clayden, J. (1998) *Going Missing*, Chichester, Wiley.

Ward, A., Kasinski, K., Pooley, J. and Worthington, A. (eds) (2003) *Therapeutic Communities for Children and Young People*. London: Jessica Kingsley.

Ward, A. (2000) Opportunity led work, Paper presented at the 1st Annual Conference of the Scottish Institute for Residential Child Care, Glasgow, 4 June 2000. Cited in Stevens, I. and Furnival, J. (2008) Therapeutic Approaches in Residential Care. In: Kendrick, A. (ed). *Residential Child Care: Prospects and Challenges*. London, Jessica Kingsley, 196–209.

Ward, H. & Munro, E. (2010) Very Young Children in Care in England: Issues for Foster Care. In Fernandez, E. and Barth, R. (eds) *How Does Foster Care Work: International Evidence on Outcomes,* London: Jessica Kingsley.

Ward, L. & Tarleton, B. (2007) Sinking and Swimming? Supporting Parents with Learning Disabilities and their children. In *Learning Disability Review*, 12(2): 22–32.

Wardhaugh, J. & Wilding, P. (1993) Towards an Explanation of the Corruption of Care. In *Critical Social Policy*, 37: 4–31.

Warner, N. (1992) *Choosing with Care: The Report of the Committee of Inquiry into the Selection, Development and Management of Staff in Children's Homes,* London, HMSO.

Waterhouse, R. (2000) *Lost in Care*: Report of the Tribunal of Inquiry into the Abuse of Children in Care in the former County Council Areas of Gwynedd and Clwyd since 1974, London: HMSO.

Welsh Assembly Government (2012) *Adoption, Outcomes and Placements for Children Looked After by Local Authorities-Year Ending 31 March 2012*, National Statistics, http://wales.gov.uk.

Whitaker, D., Archer, L. & Hicks, L. (1998) *Working in Children's Homes: Challenges and complexities,* Chichester: Wiley.

Whittaker, J. & Cressey, C. (2010) Foreword, in Fernandez, E. and Barth, R. (eds) *How Does Foster Care Work: International Evidence on Outcomes.* London: Jessica Kingsley.

Who Cares Trust (2011) *Multidimensional Treatment Foster Care-Life in care*: www.thewhocarestrust.org.uk/pages/mtfc.html

Wilkinson, R.G. and Pickett, K. (2009) *The Spirit Level,* Harmondsworth: Allen Lane.

Williams, A. (2005) New Developments in Care Planning for Children in Residential Care. In Crimmens, D., and Milligan, I. *Facing Forward: Residential Child Care in the 21st Century*, Lyme Regis: Russell House.

WMTD/Ranier/NCB (2008) *What Makes the Difference in Preparation and Planning,* London: Ranier.

Worsley, R. (2006) *Young People in Custody 2004–2006: An analysis of children's experiences of prison,* London, HMIP and YJB.

Xhou, X. and Hou, L. (1999) Children of the Cultural Revolution: the State and the life course in the People's Republic of China, *American Sociological Review,* 64:1, 12–36.

Index